TEACRAFT

BY CHARLES & VIOLET SCHAFER

ILLUSTRATED BY WIN NG

YERBA BUENA PRESS

SAN FRANCISCO

1975

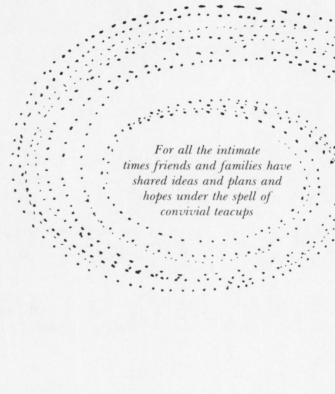

*For all the intimate
times friends and families have
shared ideas and plans and
hopes under the spell of
convivial teacups*

ISBN#0-912738-06-5

Library of Congress Card #74-14291
Printed in the United States of America
Copyright©1975 by Charles Louis Schafer and Violet Schafer
Published by Yerba Buena Press
666 Howard Street
San Francisco, California 94105

Distributed by Random House, Inc.
and in Canada by Random House of Canada, Ltd.
ISBN #394-70636-6

ABOUT THE AUTHORS

Teacraft, the third book Charles and Violet Schafer have coauthored, continues the practical and spirited approach of *Wokcraft* and *Breadcraft.*

Mr. Schafer brings firsthand knowledge of China teas from residence as an airline executive in the Orient before and after World War II. Mrs. Schafer contents herself with culinary and cultural insights gained from research and life in the United States from coast to coast.

Mr. Schafer's contagious enthusiasm for tracing and interpreting material from the far corners of the world is balanced by Mrs. Schafer's more reflective temper. He believes that to think is to act. She takes her time, saying all things need time to grow.

Both delight in the appurtenances of tea and in sharing their little house with its emphasis on handmade things. Professionally they have carved out a niche as contributors to national conference literature.

ABOUT THE ILLUSTRATOR

Win Ng's drawings for *Teacraft* embellish the fifth book in the Yerba Buena Press craft series he has illustrated.

His style ranges from lyrical and urbane to boldly inventive and humorous and takes account of many nuances in between. One must "read" his drawings to fully enjoy his eye for extraordinary details.

Mr. Ng has successfully turned his hand to clay forms, enamels, metals, water colors, collages, sculpture and fabric design. At one time or other he has exhibited and won awards in most of these media.

A gourmet, he has turned his industrial art to creating designs for tea sets with pots and matching cups and had them mass produced in Japan.

His drawings decorate posters and stationery. His advertising art is the signature of the famous Taylor & Ng department store of arts and crafts. Visitors to this store enjoy fine tea as they inspect outstanding work of craftsmen and industrial designers from around the world.

CONTENTS

MAKING MEMORIES

MAKING MEMORIES

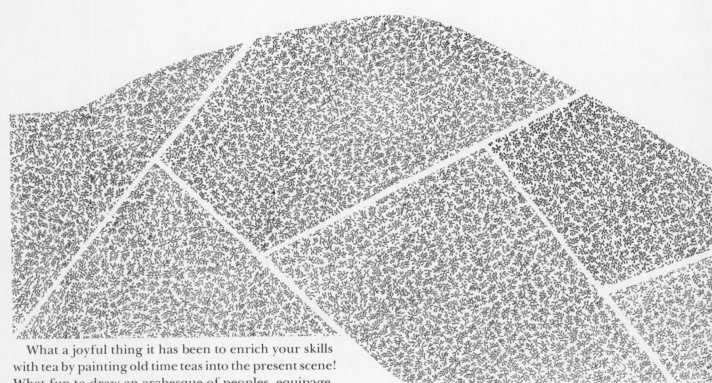

What a joyful thing it has been to enrich your skills with tea by painting old time teas into the present scene! What fun to draw an arabesque of peoples, equipage, history, folklore, delicacies and homely fare! What a challenge to be investigators, interviewers, collectors, bookworms and adventurous cooks!

Let it be said the spirit of a tea is more important than dishes and linens. Still it is a compliment to all who join you when you set a beautiful table and when you combine equal parts of love, concern and fellowship with good homemade things.

Such pleasures of tea are within easy reach. All that's required is a little time and a small boxful of recipes.

True, recipes for tea foods are not all that easy to find any more. With increasing inaccessibility of special bakeries and the disappearance of favorite cakes, cookies and breads you once could buy, it makes sense to plan to make them yourself.

Here are recipes and menus and stories for you. Fill your head with the romance of tea and your house with heady perfumes while you bake. Enjoy all day long your preparations for tea. You will make history, for your family and friends will remember you forever!

Charles and Violet Schafer
Corte Madera, California

RIVER OF JADE

Who made the first cup of tea? Who first grew tea? Who evolved its primitive manufacture? No one really knows. Tea rose out of misty and tenuous legends like some great river whose source is hardly more than a simple spring far from the sea.

We do know that China is the classical tea country. The distribution and exploitation of tea like that of jade and silk was first confined to the Celestial Empire.

We also know the Chinese word for tea. It is expressed in an ideogram that includes three symbols: *herb* 艹 ; *under cover to dry* 人 : and *picked from tree-like plant* 木 .

It is pronounced *"chah"* in Cantonese and *"tay"* in the Amoy dialect. In time the word "chah" found its way to Japan, India, Persia and Russia. "Tay" became the derivative for English "tea." Its earliest spelling was "tee" though pronounced "tay" as it was when the Dutch brought it from Java. "Tay" it was until the middle of the 18th Century even though the spelling had become "tea" as early as 1660.

TEA IN LEGEND

According to Chinese legends, the first flow of tea began quite accidentally 5,000 years ago. Tales vary. One is that the mythical philosopher-herbalist, Emperor *Shen-nung,* discovered the virtues of tea in agriculture and medicine. He was making his supper when leaves of the tea plant fell into water he was boiling and produced the first tea beverage. He found it exceedingly good and happily shared the discovery that he had found a way to make an exhilarating and fragrant drink. Tea drinking flourished thereafter.

Better to drink such a beverage, Shen-nung advised, than to drink wine which loosens the tongue. Better to drink this tea than drink unboiled water which is . infectious.

His advice was good then. It continued in force for thousands of years and into this century as botanists, explorers, travelers and missionaries have attested. Boiling water to make hot tea kept them all in good health when water supplies were impure.

Shen-nung's advice is as good today. When a parasitic ailment became epidemic among Americans visiting the Soviet Union in 1974, U.S. Public Health Service doctors warned tourists to avoid tap water in Russia. "Drink boiled water, such as tea," they advised.

TEA IN HISTORICAL TIMES

The earliest reference to tea that scholars trust is in *Erh Ya,* an ancient Chinese dictionary dating back to 350 B.C. It is believed tea was first cultivated in Szechwan and from there moved down the Yangtze Valley to the sea and from there to Japan. The first history of tea — *Ch'a Ching* written by Lu Yu about 800 A.D. — tells us that tea was a beverage in 6th Century China.

By the 7th and 8th Centuries China was the largest empire on earth. Caravans came from Persia for exotic cloth sewn of golden thread and feathers and woven gauzes as delicate as smoke.

And they came for tea. In exchange, the Chinese accepted Byzantine glass, Khotan jade, and agate and crystal from Samarkand. In China's fabled cities, the rich idled in magnificent pavilions taking tea with friends and listening to sing-song girls.

So much tea came to be grown and so much drunk by rich and poor alike that Emperor Tih-Tsung levied a tax.

In the centuries that followed, Chinese traders propagated tea from Mongolia to the Caspian Sea, from the China Sea to the Persian Gulf.

TEA CAPTURES JAPAN

The success of tea in Japan came to flower at the beginning of the 9th Century when the storied Japanese priest, Kukai, encouraged its use. A great light, they say, shone when he was born. A bright star entered his mouth in youth. He caused rain to fall. He studied in China and returned to Japan with seeds for tea plants. His tea became stimulant for student priests and medicine for the sick.

Later, there came still another priest, Eisai, with more Chinese tea seeds. He made tea drinking a ritual.

TEA OVER TRADE ROUTES

Tea was not an exclusive concern of monks and holy men. They weren't the only ones to transport seeds around the world.

For thousands of years tea was naturally dispersed over South East Asia wherever terrain was without barriers and admitted traders. Contemporary botanists in search of wild tea found a chain of tea plantations in all stages of disuse along the ancient trade routes of the Shans. These tribes of Tai stock lived in South China, Assam, Burma and Siam. They flourished from the 12th to the 16th Centuries and were largely responsible for spreading the tea bush along frontier ranges and down the long valley of the Chindwin. Wherever the Shans went, tea bushes were close by. Where tea thrived, tea drinking became habitual.

TEA OVER THE WAVES

Stories about tea appeared increasingly in Portuguese and Venetian literature during the second half of the 16th Century. At the end of that age, Englishmen had a full description of tea as a drink from a translated work by Dutch navigator, van Linschooten.

By 1606 the Dutch had opened tea plantations in Java. Four years later they were importing tea to Europe. Tea became fashionable in The Hague by 1640 and Peter Stuyvesant introduced it to North America ten years later.

According to one source, the first tea to reach England arrived with a British admiral who had discovered a small amount in the galley of a ship he captured from the Dutch.

When the Port of Canton finally opened to the white devils, tea took to the waves. In 1689, the East India Company began importing tea. Quite easily, its teas conquered England with help from Parliament which first levied less duty on its teas then on teas imported by others and then gave the company sole rights to import tea.

An agent for the company, R. L. Wickham, was the first Englishman to write of tea. In a letter from Japan, June 27, 1615, he requested a branch office to send him a "pot of the best sort of chaw."

Englishmen at this time were coffee drinkers. In a few short years they were drinking tea shipped from the Orient. The habit may have had a boost among the aristocracy when Catherine of Braganza, queen of Charles II, brought it from Portugal where it was already popular.

For years, tea came indirectly. Chinese trading junks took it to Java where the Dutch bought it and transhipped it to England and France.

A REGAL GIFT

Tea came very dear to Englishmen. For the first 100 years it was for the rich, a novelty fit for a king, as in classical times it had been the gift of Oriental emperors to their favorites.

Tea grew in popularity. London's 2,000 coffee houses were its purveyors and accepted as currency the metal and leather trade coins customarily used for small change and called "tea and coffee" tokens.

17th CENTURY ADVERTISING

On September 30, 1658, an ad in the periodical *Mercurius Politicus* offered "that excellent and by all Physitians approved China Drink called by the Chineans *Tcha*, by other nations *Tay*, alias *Tee* . . . sold at the Sultaness Head, a cophee-house in Sweetings Rents . . ."

Within a year, Thomas Garway, tobacconist, first English tea dealer and proprietor of a coffee house, had prepared a broadsheet extolling tea as a "regalia in high treatments and entertainments."

Garway charged a reasonable 15s to 50s a pound for the leaf. His coffee house also sold tea brewed according to the best recipes brought back from the Orient by merchants and travelers. It was a stimulant, he claimed, that would banish sleepiness.

TAXING TEA

From the start, tea was a convenient commodity to tax as well as to smuggle and debase. When tea drinking was ingrained, an encouraged Parliament levied eightpence a gallon on tea made or sold. This was easy to do since coffee houses made tea in large quantities and drew it off like beer. Taxing continued into modern times.

Unpopular taxes and high duties led to abuses. Foreign objects turned up in tea chests. Purveyors stained tea leaves with clay, logwood and other adulterants. A product called *smouch* and concocted of ash tree leaves boiled in copperas and sheep dung was used to debase black tea. Elder buds adulterated green tea. One small village manufactured 20 tons a year of such teas. Such infractions brought heavy fines. Nothing availed, however, until officials lowered duties.

Imports were small at first. Only finer qualities of tea entered. So great became the British demand for tea that the Chinese began to believe that the English could not live without it.

By the close of the 17th Century, imports were up to 20,000 pounds a year. In 1703, orders were out for 75,000 pounds of green; 10,000 pounds of imperial; and 20,000 pounds of bohea. Tea brought about 16s a pound.

THE SPREADING TEA GARDENS

By the close of the 18th Century, the East India Company monopoly was promoting teas from China and India for sale in England and colonial America. Despite challenges from other European colonial powers which sought to propagate tea in their African and American possessions, the East India Company dominated the tea trade. To maintain its superior position, as it did for almost 200 years, the company also cast about for ways to grow tea, expedite shipment and smash competitors.

Tea traders enlisted botanist-explorers to collect plants and seeds; naval architects to design faster ships; and, it was suspected, medical men to praise the leaf.

An early raid on guarded tea gardens in China was the goal of a young Dutch tea taster. He managed to bring back tea seeds as well as laborers to cultivate tea plants in the Dutch East Indies. So began the tea industry of Indonesia.

In 1843, Robert Fortune, a Scotch botanist, talked his way into the forbidden interior of China disguised as a Chinese in order to collect plants and seeds from tea plantations. In the process, he uncovered the Chinese secret that green tea was not from a plant different from that which produced black tea. It was the process that made the difference.

He also brought back the curious legend of the tea monkeys. In the sacred hills of Bohea where tea grew in inaccessible places, he was told that monkeys did the harvesting. These lazy animals would not normally do this; so when they were far up where the tea bushes grew, the Chinese threw stones at them. The angry monkeys retaliated by tearing off branches of the tea bushes and hurling them at their attackers.

Botanical hassles developed. One of them tragically delayed recognition and acceptance of the native tea plants in Assam. Imported Chinese tea plants and Chinese methods proved inappropriate in India.

TEA IS DANDY!

It was hinted that the East India Company inspired Dr. Cornelius Bontekoë of the University of Leyden to write a glowing treatise on *The Most Excellent Herb, Tea*. Water, it said, was comfortless, but tea was dandy since drinking it incurred no shame of intemperance. Tea also remedied heaviness of spirit and cured colds.

TEA NAVIES

All the time, the British of all classes and conditions were drinking tea despite the expense. Their habit was maintained largely because of the supremacy of the British seamen who transported the tea and the merchants who had thousands of outlets at which to sell tea. Enough was available for everyone in England to have tea once a day.

Transporting tea was a game of calculated risks. Commercial rivalry and international jealousies launched hundreds of ships. The East India Company had a fleet of giant armed "tea-waggons" and fought their way through the Portuguese to the Indian coast. They defied the Dutch. The East Indiamen, as they were called, were triple threats: merchant ship, passenger vessel and man-of-war.

IMPORT BY STEALTH

Nor did all the tea from the Orient ride the waves to a snug harbor in the British Isles. Smuggling and hijinks added a wicked sense of peril to enjoyment of the brew.

Taxes on tea gave freetraders, as they were called, a profit of 350 percent to work with. Smuggling was actually an industry. It employed thousands. Boats stood off shore with fleets of dinghies bobbing alongside to deliver tea in the black of night. Furtive signals from shore showed that the "coast was clear." Oarlocks creaked in hidden bays.

There was hardly a man, woman, child or conniving innkeeper in the surrounding countryside who would not help conceal tea in caves, deep cellars and church crypts once it was ashore. Highwaymen on horseback posted tea to clandestine buyers anywhere in the country. Pack horses and strings of pony carts galloped through the night loaded with tea. Duffers padded themselves with as much as 100 pounds of tea on a single carry. For a price, local shepherds drove their flocks over telltale tracks left on sandy beaches by passing gangs. So many carters were at work smuggling that a shortage of farm labor existed in some districts.

Highborn ladies had no qualms about writing friends outside England to smuggle in tea. Smugglers made purchases directly from captains. Even reputable merchants dealt in contraband tea. People of wealth and officials as well enjoyed smuggled tea. Commoners generally applauded. No moral stigma attached to the traffic.

HALF THE TEA IN ENGLAND

Things were so far out of hand that tea was displacing ale. This cut into the malt tax. "A terrible situation," protested an M.P. "Tea drugs and debases workingclass women!"

As he spoke, half the tea in England was being smuggled in. Revenuers managed to recapture vast shipments. In 1733, this amounted to 54,000 pounds. Still, hijackers outwitted them, repossessing tea by resorting to shootouts and fast horses.

RECKLESS MISCHIEF

Skippers and offloaders alike lived out long and perilous careers, and grim were the reprisals against informers. Hundreds of witnesses to smuggling shut their eyes to derringdo for fear of losing their lives.

Captured smugglers were often pressed into the British navy unless they chose jail. Many were killed, their tombstones bearing witness to their lives in pursuit of the shady business. Smuggling lost its profit and lure only when Pitt repealed high duties and compelled the East India Company to import enough to drive the price down.

ENTER THE YANKEE CLIPPERS

In time, repeal of the British navigation acts permitted American ships to enter the tea trade. Speed and power took precedence over tonnage, allowing naval architects to design a new kind of vessel to rush tea from China to England by way of the Cape of Good Hope. These first tea clippers evolved from the swift privateers built in Baltimore for the War of 1812. Their radically different design and hard-driving captains ushered in one of the most romantic decades in maritime history.

The tea clipper, *Rainbow,* was so fast she was first to bring news back to New York of her arrival in Canton! *Sea Witch,* launched in 1846, broke more records than any ship her size and established world records in the China trade.

PATTERN FOR THE BRITISH

Oriental, first American clipper to arrive in the port of London, created a tremendous stir. Carrying a cargo of 1600 tons of tea, she commanded twice the rate other ships could charge. Her owners asked $48,000 in freight money for the run — two-thirds the cost of building the ship.

This spurred the English. Almost before the *Oriental* cleared for home, they had laid the keel for the first of their own China clippers.

The *Cairngorm*, built in 1853, was the first to equal American clipper ships in speed. She and the *Sea Witch* vied in carrying tea from China to London.

GREAT TEA RACE PHOTO FINISH

Each year tea clippers raced home to collect the premium for the first cargo to sell at auction in Mincing Lane. Captains and crews were the best. Public interest was so high citizens placed bets. Winner of this marine derby was the one who first hurled sample boxes of tea ashore to waiting clerks who drew samples and rushed them to Mincing Lane. Handsome cash rewards went to victorious captains and crews.

The last of the great tea races took place in 1867. Nine competing British clippers started at Foochow, China, almost simultaneously. Three crossed the final bar in company 99 days later. They had covered 16,000 miles and put in at different docks in London within two hours of each other. Clippers *Taeping* and *Ariel* tied.

Then all the romance died with the opening of the Suez Canal and the advent of steamships.

TEA, THE IMMIGRANT

From England, of course, tea had long since traveled to the American colonies. American colonists drank tea in great quantities. They drank it at wakes. Madam Winthrop had the distinction of serving tea after a lecture. It was customary to drink tea for breakfast if one could afford it. Only diehard beer and cider types maligned tea as poisonous, base and exotic.

Then the English Parliament erred. Thinking, perhaps, that what was good for the East India Company was good for Britain, it passed the Tea Act of 1773. Resentful Americans began a squabble that gave tea a bad image hardly erased to this day.

Tories kept on drinking tea when they could smuggle it in as snuff or tobacco. Other colonists substituted

Liberty Teas. These they brewed from four-leaved loosestrife, Labrador tea, balm, ribwort, sage, and leaves of currant and raspberry.

Patriots, students, children and women took the pledge. A poetess publicly bade farewell to her teacups, saucers, cream jug, sugar tongs and pretty tea chest.

AN UNFORGETTABLE DISTURBANCE

As public anger against the tax increased, so did ugly incidents. The most dramatic was the Boston Tea Party. On December 13, 1773, colonials armed with hatchets and pistols broke open and dumped into Boston Harbor 342 chests of tea valued at £10,000.

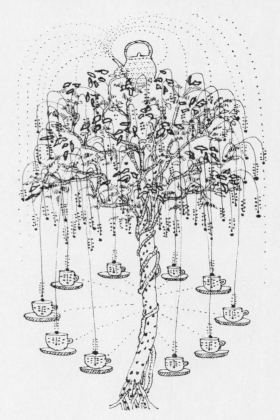

King George II fulminated, "The die is now cast. The colonies must either submit or triumph."

A disapproving George Washington nevertheless responded, ". . . Americans will never be taxed without their own consent, . . . the cause of Boston . . . now is and ever more will be considered as the cause of America . . ."

AN ELOQUENT OKAY FOR THE TEA PARTY

A most eloquent expression of the importance of the Tea Party came from John Adams.

This is the most magnificent Movement of all. There is a Dignity, a Majesty, and Sublimity, in this last effort of the Patriots, that I greatly admire. The people should never rise, without doing something to be remembered – something notable, and striking. This destruction of the Tea is so bold, so daring, so firm, intrepid and inflexible, and it must have so important Consequences, and so lasting, that I can't but consider it as an Epocha in History.

Not long after, the American War of Independence was joined.

TEA TODAY

The tenuous River of Jade that rose out of the mists 5,000 years ago has flowed over the seas and become a sea itself. It continues to be a brew to reckon with.

In Boston in 1973, occasion presented itself to celebrate the bicentennial of the Boston Tea Party.

There was to be a boat, some tea and some folks dressed as Indians who would throw the tea into the water. But Indians protested that such plans defiled their image. According to their research, colonials had

not dressed as Indians. They had merely pulled blankets over their heads and painted their faces black, not red.

Boston planners suggested a compromise.

Next, the Americanism officer of the local Disabled American Veterans claimed the right to stage the event. His organization had celebrated the Tea Party for six years, he declared. "No one tells us how to do it."

Following him came the People's Bicentennial Commission. "Government sponsored celebrations of the nation's bicentennial are a travesty of the American revolutionary myth," said its spokesman. "We intend to sail our own boat from New York into Boston Harbor, do battle with the Boston boat and see who deserves the honor of conducting the tea party."

Finally, the Sierra Club protested tea would pollute the waters. This enraged the veterans who had a gift of 500 pounds of tea from a tea company. The tea company coolly retired "under a commitment to ecology."

To satisfy all, Boston ended with three events. As it happens, no one could have thrown tea onto the exact spot the colonists used. Where tea chests once bobbed defiantly, autos now roar by on an expressway.

A WORLDWIDE, LASTING AFFAIR

Tea has lost none of its power to stimulate or evoke emotional responses. Raise its price in the marketplace and housewives in England go on the warpath and write scathing letters to the editor.

Levy an unpopular tax in Connecticut and a taxpayer's association sends tea bags to state legislators to remind them of American traditions in regard to uncontrolled taxation.

Let the new governor of Baluchistan ban tea drinking in government offices as a waste of time, and masses of tea peons, canteen and tea stall operators are thrown out of work. Intolerable!

Let the president of an Oriental country railroad a bill that allows him to run for a third term, and opposition senators and deputies hurl teacups in anger.

The rivers of jade are indeed deep and very wide and the story of tea is hardly told.

FOLKLORE, FOLK MEDICINE

MIRACLE OF THE EYELIDS

A Japanese tale describes the wonderful origin of tea in China. Bodhidharma — Indian prince and Buddhist saint — appeared in China to spread the doctrines of Gautama. He resolved to sit before a wall in meditation for nine years. During one of his meditations, he fell asleep and was so mortified at commission of this sin that he cut off his eyelids. Cast to the ground, they miraculously took root at once and grew into tea plants. The leaves, steeped in hot water, made the tea that killed sleep.

SYMBOLIC AND SPECIAL USES

Whatever its origin, tea symbolizes the waters of life and eternal wakefulness for the Chinese. On numerous occasions they make special use of it.

Boat people include ceremonial teas as part of weddings. They also dress their temple altars with fruit, flowers and heaps of red packets containing tea. On leaving, temple visitors receive a packet, for they believe tea has healing powers.

Tea eases the path to purgatory. In the seventh week after death, the soul enters the realm of the Prince of the Wheel and there petitions to expedite his transmigration. A rest house provides tea for him. A virtuous soul finds the tea comforting, cool and refreshing. An evil doer can only expect the tea to erase all memory of his past.

TIME-TO-GO TEA

Tea is a social signal for the Chinese. Above all other races, they are connoisseurs of food. At banquets they discuss food more than they socialize. When the last dish is removed, tea and fruit appear to signal that the party is over. Only minutes remain for polite farewells and congratulation of the host.

TIMING BY THE TEACUP

The Chinese language is vague about time. In early days, few establishments kept the time. Watches and clocks in Treaty Ports were largely ignored. Expression of time was tied to familiar activities like the boiling of a teakettle or the drinking of a cup of tea.

TEA FOR PILGRIMS

Long ago an annual celebration in Peking included a pilgrimage to the Marvelous Peak in the Western Hills. During the Peony Moon, religious devotees went joyously forth. Wealthy merchant and donkey boy alike marched off to climb until there was nothing between them and the sky.

As each passed a shrine along the way, yea, even a dog, an attendant registered his passage with the stroke of a gong to tell the gods that another worshipper was on his way to acquiring merit. And for all, there was free, hot tea in mat sheds manned by philanthropic societies.

& FORTUNES

TEA FOR HUNGRY GHOSTS

The Cantonese Hungry Ghosts Festival featured tea and the King of Hell. Appropriate rites took place to dissuade neglected or disappointed ghosts from haunting the community in the year ahead.

Everyone contributed to the celebration. Little banks of sand appeared in the main street for prayerful burning of incense, bundles of paper clothing and ingots representing gold and silver. Those rich enough contributed lighted candles and cups of tea. Priests presided while lay helpers filled tea and wine cups in sand castles from pots on the altar.

HOLY TEA WATER

A paper junk provisioned with tea, wine and oil was consigned to the water.

In a final ceremony, ghosts received rations of tea, rice and vegetables. Standing before a table laid with musical instruments, a bowl of tea and a wooden shrine, the priest produced from his robes a white paper charm sealed in red. He folded it, set it afire and let the ashes drop into the tea bowl. Then he drew the bowl to himself to impart magic properties.

The symbolic distribution of food and money followed. Making mystic signs to north, east, south and west and over the consecrated tea bowl, the priest moved his hand counterclockwise for the first time in the ceremonies. In benediction, he dipped his fingers in the tea and sprinkled it over the congregation. The tea bowl was then delivered to the senior elder.

The ghosts, thus appeased, returned to the underworld.

THE LAST TEA

Ceremonial teas follow Chinese burial masses. After such a tea, the senior lady stations herself by a tray containing lucky money in red paper wraps. She hands a packet to each mourner. The deceased also shares in the distribution.

MAGIC, MEDICINE AND COOKERY

All over the world, teas originate with herbs, flowers, leaves, bark, seeds, roots, grains and even fresh meat. Their use extends from magic to medicine. Some teas are valued simply for their taste, bouquet and glow in the cup.

FOR HEALTH'S SAKE

Beef tea received special attention from early cooks here and abroad. Cookbooks indexed it under *Invalid or Convalescent Cookery.* An old English text gave rules for "ordinary beef tea," "quickly made beef tea," and "raw beef tea," to be served in a tinted glass "to disguise the color."

Dr. Chase, the garrulous 19th Century physician and avid recipe hunter, refused to trick anyone with colored glasses, but he did advise adding wine.

BROIL A NICE STEAK

Dr. Chase suggested beef tea makers broil steak from which all fat was removed. Then place the steak, he said, in a bowl of hot water. Press it until all the juices and strength are extracted. Repeat until steak has nothing more to give. Cut into inch-size squares and press with a lemon squeezer. This produces an extract that looks like wine.

When the chemistry of protein cookery caught up with Dr. Chase, he tried steeping. He felt a special need to share his recipe with his millions of readers after noting the astronomical price of $1.25 for a two-ounce bottle of beef tea extract. His recipe read:

Take ⅓ lb. fresh beef, mutton, poultry or game (lean part only), minced very fine; place it in 14 ozs. soft cold water (2 or 3 tbsps. less than 1 pt.) to which has been added a pinch or about 18 grs. of table salt, and 3 or 4 drops of muriatic acid; stir all with a wooden spoon (on account of the acid, which rusts iron) and set it aside for 1 hr., stirring it occasionally; then strain it through gauze, or a sieve, and wash the residue left on the sieve by means of 5 additional ozs. of cold soft water, pressing it so that all soluble matter will be removed from the residue; mix the 2 strainings and the extract is ready for use. It should be drunk freely every 2 or 3 hours.

EVIL TEAS

In the 17th and 18th Centuries, practitioners of obeah in the Caribbean had a formidable knowledge of the properties of plants. They made teas from leaves, bark and berries to cure or kill. From bones and teeth taken from a grave, an obeah man could boil a tea that would dispatch a victim by the ninth day.

OMNIBUS TEA BATH

Not all magic teas were bad. It is said an overseer's daughter in the West Indies took a tea bath to cure an unsightly skin condition. Precisely at midnight, she got into the witches' brew to the tune of Christian incantations.

The tea bath recipe, given to a local obeah man in a dream, listed lemon grass, horehound, limes, olive bush, soursop leaves, circe bush, honeysuckle, guava, cowfoot, sage, jack-in-the-bush, thistle, elder, bitter tally, cochineal, duppy basil, grape, and ringworm bush. They were steeped in rain and seawater. From one of the ingredients is brewed a homemade phenobarbitol.

HERBAL TEA REMEDIES

Thousands in Yugoslavia and elsewhere drink teas made from herbs, flowers, and leaves, thinking to cure everything from swollen joints to arteriosclerosis. A controversial pharmácy in Belgrade deals exclusively in folk remedies. Cost is small — from 25 to 45 cents for three ounces. In 1972, people from all walks of life bought 200,000 boxes of these teas.

On the Greek Island of Kos, black-shawled grandmothers in mountain villages practice medicine much as they did in Hippocrates' day. They boil special herbs over twig fires to make teas for treating colds, depression and lovesickness.

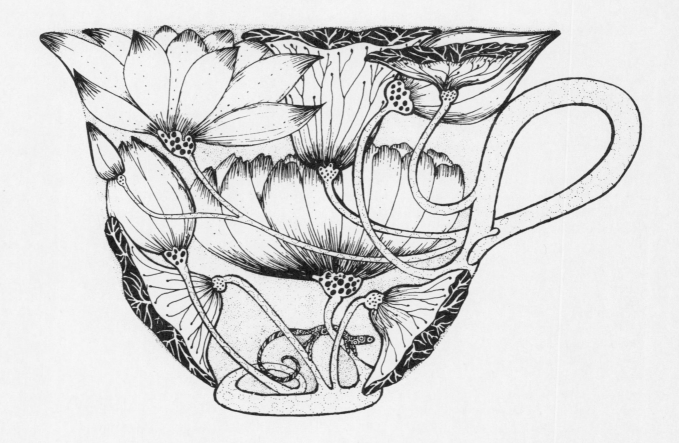

CHINESE HERBAL TEAS

Outstripping all others are the Chinese herb doctors. Their austere shops are floor-to-ceiling pantries full of drawers with herbs by the hundreds. The herbalist knows the exact location of each.

To get his advice, you describe your symptoms and give your age. He may take your pulse, check your tongue and prescribe a tea to be made from 10 to 15 herbs.

Herb doctors operate on the principle that sickness results from imbalances in the body. Health depends on harmony between two opposing but complementary forces—the cool and hot or the *yin* and *yang*. When you eat too many hot foods, such as fried chicken, nuts and potato chips, you restore the body's balance with teas.

The herbalist may prescribe a dozen dried grasses, roots, bark, leaves or insects. Some quantities he judges by hand; others he weighs carefully on a delicate hand scale. He uses mortar and pestle to break up solids for easier brewing. He slices ginger root by hand.

He places all on a piece of paper, folds it to close, and tallies cost on his abacus. He tells you how to make the tea. "Use two bowls of water and boil until only one is left. Drink before retiring." He gives you a sweet to offset his unpleasant cure.

HERB TEA FOR A COLD

Our Man's faith in Chinese herbal cures has a practical basis. During the Japanese occupation of Hong Kong, he saw Chinese hospitals in action, successfully serving the public even though all Western medicines had been confiscated. Chinese herbs, some boiled all day long, were their mainstay.

It was natural, years later, to accept the gift of a Chinese friend's herbal cure for a cold. The herbs came in an attractive cardboard box papered with a happy red and white all-over design. The box opened on a paper hinge. On it was the legend:

LAM CHON CHAR, Composed of Chinese Herbs
Indications: Use as beverage to soothe dry membranes of throat. Active Ingredients:

Olives	30%	Olive leaves, chopped
Soo-Ip	40%	Perilla Ceimoides (Asiatic mint)
Sang-Chung	30%	Licorice root, chopped

Directions: 1 tablespoon added to 3 cups boiling water. Let stand for 1 hour in a covered vessel, strain and drink a teacupful morning and evening. If relief is not obtained, see your doctor. For children use proportionately less.

Our friend suggested boiling green onions in a pint of water for a half hour before adding the herbs. The house reeked of the onion, and when the herbs went in, what a wicked black brew it was! But the cure worked. Our Man woke the next morning with no trace of his cold.

DIVINING TEA

Just as Scotch Highlanders read tea leaves at breakfast to get ready for the day ahead—to get an idea what to expect—a letter, a parcel, visitors, perhaps—so we have amused ourselves reading leaves. At least the clairvoyant member of the family has done so. In fact, he proposed by reading my teacup. He saw in it a lady, dressed to the nines and wearing a flamboyant hat. She was making an announcement, he said, of great importance to herself and of great pleasure to an applauding audience of women! How like a man to consider his proposal the occasion for so ecstatic a reception! Let that be, though, for it all turned out well.

LONG DISTANCE FORTUNE

A skeptic once asked, "Can you read my cup if I am not present?"

"Certainly," said Our Man. "Drink a cup of tea tonight at 8:00. I will have one, too. Make a wish, and I will read your fortune in my cup."

So it happened. We both laughed merrily when we inspected the cup. "Our friend is going on an unexpected business trip," we agreed. In the cup was a frantic man with coattails flying and traveling bags. He was bidding his wife and children a rushed goodbye.

All was reported the next morning. "Stuff and nonsense," said our friend. "I never go anywhere, certainly not on business, and not in a hurry."

At 3:00 that afternoon, he called. "You and your darned tea leaves! Do you know what has just happened? I have to leave early and fly to New Jersey tonight!"

EXCITING LANGUAGE OF TEA

Few things elicit more rapt attention or invest social encounter with more delicious anticipation than fortune telling with tea leaves. Non-tea drinkers suddenly develop a taste for it.

A whole dictionary of symbols surrounds the art. One can read a book to learn how to interpret them. Yet we think imagination, showmanship and genuine empathy are of the greatest value. If it isn't fun, it is better untried.

READING TEA LEAVES

This is how one tea leaf reader works. First, he puts coarse, black tea in the teapot for brewing. He always uses black tea because it produces bold pictures. When the subject who is to have his fortune told has drunk his fill, the reader takes his cup. If too few leaves remain and there is little liquid, he adds a teaspoon of leaves from the pot and a little tea.

He asks the subject to make a secret wish. This establishes a solemn mood even though it is always understood that the session is just for fun.

Taking the cup in both hands so that it faces away from him, the reader holds it directly over the saucer and slowly rotates it, tipping it gradually so that the liquid trickles out slowly. The cup ends upside down on the saucer.

The reader does not see what is happening to the leaves as they are distributed around the inside of the cup, but those opposite him can see what is happening.

The reader leaves the cup on the saucer briefly to let the last drops drain out.

"Have you made your wish?" he asks.

"At this point I feel it necessary to psych myself," he says. "It helps if the subject is not openly skeptical. I try to sense whether all the signs are right even though the tea leaves have already formed the shapes I will read when I turn the cup upright. During this pause, I sometimes feel like a conduit for insight and hazard being clairvoyant by telling the subject his wish will come true.

"Then I turn the cup and, talking fast, voice my first impressions.

WHAT TEA LEAVES TELL

"I look for realistic shapes — animals, birds, everday utensils, outlines of maps — and assign meaning to their placement, symbolism and applications to the subject's immediate situation and future activities. Since much is to be guessed, I ask if it's possible leaves mean this or that or something else. I don't force answers.

"I keep turning the cup, looking at it upside down, as it were, to see what other pictures emerge. This I interpret as a secondary fortune.

"As I explore each facet, I share it with those around the table so that they can verify my observations. 'Here is a man. There is a duck,' and so on.

"More than sheer chance seems involved in the way tea leaves are distributed. Almost invariably, persons whose lives are well ordered show cups with clear pictures. Those whose lives are chaotic show scattered cups. Teacups seem to mirror indecision or great purpose. It is sometimes disturbing to discover that a fortune approached as social entertainment is an accurate prediction."

CURES & CONTROVERSIES

EXHILARATING TO SAY THE LEAST

One of the most popular non-alcoholic stimulants is tea. Half the world enjoys it. Chemically, it contains caffeine and tannin. Ingested individually, these substances are harsh.

Caffeine is stimulating. Tea leaves contain more of it than do coffee beans, but infusing them produces a relatively mild brew. A six-ounce cup of tea has about 90mg. of caffeine to coffee's 150mg.

Tannin gives tea its taste and astringency. Tea drinkers often remove the latter quality by using milk. This has no effect on taste but does add ten calories to the four already in a cup of black tea. It should be added that tea tannin is not the tannic acid that tans leather.

FIRST A MEDICINE

Tea as medicine predated tea as a common beverage. To people of the Yangtse-Kiang Valley, tea was a medicine before it became a beverage in the 5th Century. In the 8th Century, the blind Chinese priest, Ganjin, arrived in Japan with medicines. One of these was tea. Temple priests in succeeding centuries prepared tea as medicine for the masses and student priests, observing tea's capacity to overcome drowsiness, incorporated tea drinking in their course of study.

What kind of tea this was is not known, but it was probably old Chinese brick tea formed by steaming leaves together. The Chinese chewed it as they drank hot water. They also made a paste of it to alleviate pain of rheumatism. The Japanese ground it to powder instead and mixed it with hot water to make a drink.

THIS PRODUCT WILL CURE . . .

New discoveries often enjoy extravagant puffs. Early tea was no exception.

An ancient legend credits tea with curing alcoholism. A Chinese gentleman in the 5th Century observed that tea leaves when they fell into pools left an orange tinge and bitter taste. After tasting it, he dismissed it as too acrid to drink.

Then it occurred to him that it might discourage alcoholism. His method was simply to drown his patient internally with it. "If I keep him full of this harsh stuff," he reasoned, "he will have no room for alcohol." The cure worked.

London tea dealer Thomas Garway declared teas preserved health until extreme old age. Tea, he said, "helpeth the headache, giddiness and heaviness thereof, removeth obstructions of the spleen, is very good against stone and gravel, taketh away the difficulty of breathing, opening obstructions, is good against lippitude distillations and cleareth the eyesight."

Do "lippitude distillations" shock you? They need not. They are simply evidence of bleareyedness.

TEA, A FIGHTING WORD

Even as Garway was blowing a horn for tea, others strongly denied its benefits. A great protest rose from preachers and writers. Tea injured health, they charged. It threatened public order and undermined the morals of the working class.

Philanthropist Jonas Hanway published "*An Essay on Tea*; considered as pernicious to Health; obstructing industry; and impoverishing the Nation." A roving British commentator lamented that money wasted on tea was better spent on bread and he deplored the time lost coming and going to the tea table.

Reformer John Wesley denounced tea as an evil to body and soul. Time mitigated his rage and he became such a confirmed tea drinker that Josiah Wedgwood created a two-quart teapot for him to use for Sunday breakfasts.

In spite of critics, tea drinking continued to spread and the tea trade made profits huge enough to cover all ships and cargoes the East India Company lost at sea.

EVERYWHERE A CRITIC

Critics in France were vitriolic. Tea never caught on there and was tagged as insipid and perilous. Historian Legrand D'Aussy spread rumors that the Dutch East India Company bribed physicians to praise tea.

Controversy raged in medical circles. English and Dutch doctors claimed that new diseases had broken out and old maladies had increased in frequency when tea drinking became habitual.

Balzac, lumping tea with alcohol, coffee, sugar and tobacco, warned that their sudden coming into excessive use threatened to change society.

Occasionally a doctor would hail tea for its stimulating effect. Such was Lémery, physician to Louis XIV. He gave tea good marks for refreshing the spirit and curing headaches, provided one limited his intake to 10 or 12 cups a day!

PERISH THE NAUGHTY STUFF!

When Dr. William Alcott put his mind to the tea problem in the 1830s, he outdid Balzac. He judged tea as evil as opium and was outraged by wicked attempts to grow tea in the United States. He poured out streams of essays to preach the good way to a healthy life. This did not include imbibing tea.

His little volume, *Tea and Coffee*, published in 1839, has a very long and specific catalogue of tea sins. It charged:

Tea is a national and individual waste. It is properly and strictly a medicine. It is intoxicating. It is poison, etc., etc.

Dr. Alcott marshalled every kind of argument, even to charging that people were wrecking their teeth by drinking tea. This has been disputed by a contemporary British dental research team that claims tea is as good for teeth as fluoridated water.

One of Dr. Alcott's most fascinating arguments concerned tea's sinful waste.

Everyone who pursues a course of tea drinking not only expends – at six dollars a year – this large sum, but he is also accessory, by his example, to the expenditure of the same sum by many others. We are creatures of imitation. The example of every individual has its influence on other individuals. If tea drinking is a national sin, and if the consumption, in the United States of $20 million worth of tea yearly is not only a national sin but a national waste, to say nothing more of it at present, is not everyone who uses tea at all more or less involved in the guilt of this great national waste?

Think of the good it could do – support 50,000 families; employ 50,000 teachers; support 30,000 preachers – 50 - 60 times as many foreign missionaries . . . .

He computed the compound interest for these sums. In 40 years, he said, tea could fill the Great Western Canal in New York twice. And, he added, there wasn't even an excuse for tea anywhere in the Bible. Tea drinking was tyranny and tea drinkers were not even good citizens, he concluded.

MODERATION IN ALL THINGS

Not all doctors agreed with him. John Lettsom, a famous English physician, observed that the universal habit allowed everyone to judge for himself whether tea affected health. He advised that "tea if not drunk too hot nor in too great quantities is perhaps preferable to any other vegetable infusion."

TEA AS A TREATMENT

At the opening of the 20th Century, a physician's receipt book listed more tea items in its medical index than in its index of cooking recipes. Under *"Food for the Sick,"* it pointed out:

A rather weak tea (never a strong one) may be made of any of the ordinary green or black teas, when craved by the sick, sweetening and using milk as desired; for we believe it better to allow a mild beverage of this kind to any sick person rather than to allow their minds to worry over a refusal, for all excitement is to be avoided if reasonably possible, for amendment seldom begins, nor does it continue long, after any dissatisfaction arises, no matter what the subject, nor how slight the dissatisfaction may be; hence indulge all opinions, or even whims, that have not in themselves an absolute wrong.

WHAT'S GOOD FOR THE MASTER . . . .

Even a dog can benefit from tea. Hansie, an elegant dachshund of our acquaintance, owed his recovery from a wasting illness to tea. His veterinarian prescribed "tea as strong as you can make it and with as much sugar as can be dissolved in it. Force Hansie's jaws open and spoon it in every 15 minutes. The sugar will give him strength and the tannin will sooth his stomach."

ANOTHER TEA CURE

Resourceful housewives from Colonial days on have treated their families with teas made from corn, herbs, roots, seeds and leaves.

They brewed tea from dried field corn they had carefully browned in the oven and ground like coffee

beans. Over a cup of ground corn, they poured a pint of boiling water and let it steep. The tea was mild enough for a delicate stomach.

PHARMACY OF THE FIELDS

Native Indians and pioneers found teas in their fields and kitchen gardens.

Chamomile flower tea, dubbed "garden physician," was valued as a mild and soothing tonic. Borage tea was for non-drinkers who wanted to feel exhilarated. Catnip, rich in vitamins A and C, was a popular panacea for infant ills and a valued sleep inducer.

Sage tea was a sore throat gargle. Mint tea settled stomachs. Pennyroyal tea broke up colds that threatened after exposure.

Tonic teas came from roots of gentian, sassafras, burdock, sarsaparilla, yellow dock and licorice.

Strawberry leaf tea cured babies with mouth cankers and supplied grownups with gargles. Blackberry and raspberry teas were specifics for bowel complaints.

Roasted chicory root produced a tea that tasted like coffee but lacked the caffeine.

The list of teas could go on forever.

TEA RECIPES WITH SPIRIT AND SPIRITS

Teas of green mint, peppermint and spearmint each enjoyed special functions. Sometimes they were juleped, laced with wine or brandy and pounded ice. Quickly drunk, they promised to produce the agreeable sensation of a hailstorm in the neighborhood.

The everlasting plant, recommended for coughs, was boiled with figs, raisins and licorice and served with lemon. Since it was innocent, one could drink it freely.

For nervous wrecks, one made tea with two parts hawthorn to one part each of sage and balm. Some claimed that meadow hay was as much superior to the "dried leaves of China, as gold and silver are superior to copper and lead." It was said to make a spirited tea for breakfast and a quieting one at day's end. Betony, gathered just before flowering, made a tea to cure headaches.

OTHER STIMULATING TEA CONCOCTIONS

Caudles, warm drinks made especially for invalids, often contained China tea. A pre-Civil War receipt required a pint of strong green tea, kept warm over a slow fire. Stirred into the tea were the yolks of two well beaten eggs, a cup of white wine, a grating of nutmeg and sugar to taste. The tea was reheated and served at once.

A tea punch from the same era required two ounces of hyson and one ounce of good black tea infused with three quarts of boiling water. Into that went enough spirits and sugar to invigorate if not intoxicate, there being a pint of rum and five of brandy. It was not Emily Post's kind of tea punch, but it must have generated lively talk.

REST AND REHABILITATION TEA

The best use for tea is to help people relax. Tea affects the central nervous system. Its caffeine content is said to produce a clearer flow of thought, to allay fatigue, and to encourage sustained intellectual effort. Reaction time shortens.

A medical researcher for the United States Air Force recently stated, "Tea is as good an agent for the relief of fatigue as has yet been discovered. In an age when man travels faster, farther, higher and deeper; concocts the biggest bang and the brightest flash of light; produces more material goods; and plays harder than ever conceived possible in the wildest dreams of eras past, it is quite possible that tea time is what a man needs most to enable him to find respite from his fatigue, anxiety and tension states."

QUEEN OF THE CAMELLIAS, PRETENDERS & RIVALS

Tea is indigenous to China, Tibet and Northern India. It grows in Assam, Java, Formosa, Sri Lanka (formerly Ceylon). It has been attempted in other places including South Carolina. Chief exporters are India and Sri Lanka.

Some historians and herbalists have thought the tea plant was native, not to China, but to India and so gave rise to legends. But contemporaries think the teas may have had separate origins, India tea coming from wild plants near the source of the Irrawaddy in Assam or Northern Burma; the China, coming from China.

There are large leafed India teas and China teas with narrow, hardier leaves.

QUEEN OF THE CAMELLIAS

Tea is kin to the ornamental camellia but now has a generic status of its own as *Thea sinensis*. Propagation is from seed only. The finest teas are produced at high elevations. A well cared for bush will live more than 50 years. Botanists have described many varieties but are not generally agreed on the number. This is partly because tea's character is affected by the place it grows.

Tea is an evergreen, shrubby in form. Growing freely in nature, unpruned and unplucked, it soars 30 feet and bears waxen, roselike white blossoms. To maintain a manageable height, tea planters prune tea to three to five feet.

Commercial teas circle the earth at or near the equator. The finest grow in mountains to 6,000 feet. Tea likes neither frost nor hot and humid plains. The Chinese have cultivated it commercially since the beginning of the Christian era, the Japanese since 800 A.D.

As with common garden plants, pests bedevil tea. At least one pest is benign. In India's Darjeeling district the green fly that attacks and stunts tea leaves makes it one of the world's best teas.

CULTIVATING TEA

Tea grows in gardens and plantations, starting out in nursery beds. Plants are transplanted when they are six to eight inches and set in well spaced rows in order to get the fullest exposure to sun. On a tea estate in Sri Lanka, each plant has an allotted 12 square feet of surface soil. This gives a fully planted acre about 3630 tea plants.

When plants are four to six feet, they are cut back to encourage plucking and convenience in harvesting. By the end of the third year, tea is ready to pick. By the tenth year, tea plants are full bearing and can yield as much as a quarter pound of tea in several flushes a season.

Time of plucking depends on elevation. In low country, from sea level to 2,000 feet, tea plants mature in two years. Harvesters pluck by hand or use special shears. The younger the leaf, the finer the quality.

TENDER LEAF

For a delicate quality, pluckers take only the bud and two extreme leaves of each shoot. For a large yield, they pluck as many as four leaves from the top of the shoot down. They leave the eye or bud in the axil of the leaf to encourage lateral buds and fresh plucking within ten days.

Pluckers, carrying baskets suspended by ropes from their heads, toss leaves over their shoulders into the baskets. These baskets hold 14 pounds. At the end of each row is a transport basket for pluckings. About 3200 leaves make a pound and 30,000 constitute a good day's plucking. Women are preferred for this work.

FLAVOR VARIES

Flavor and quality of tea vary with climate, soil, age of leaf, time of harvest and even from year to year. Flavor also varies from hill to hill, from growth in sun or shade. Dry days and cool nights produce top quality.

In Dimbula, one of Sri Lanka's tea districts, the climate is perfect. The formation of the hills ensures

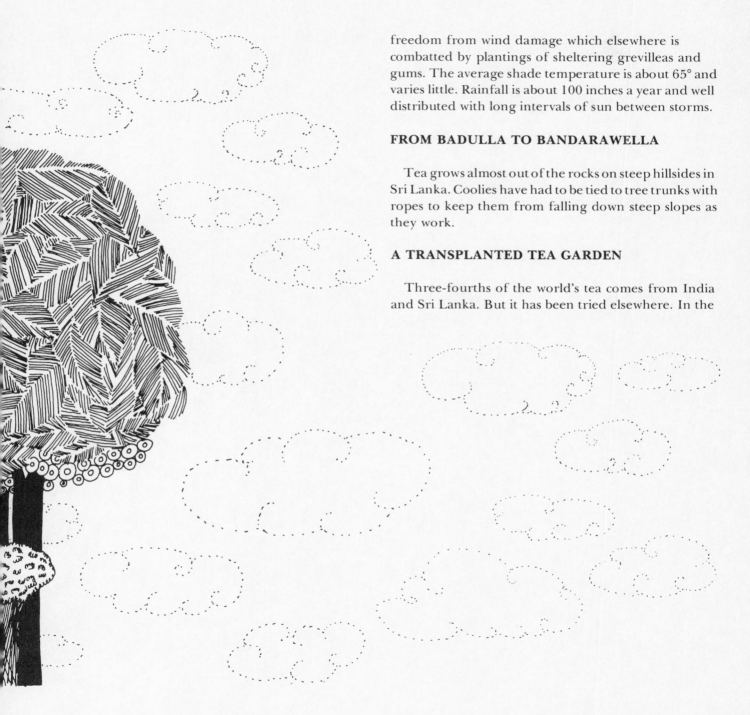

freedom from wind damage which elsewhere is combatted by plantings of sheltering grevilleas and gums. The average shade temperature is about 65° and varies little. Rainfall is about 100 inches a year and well distributed with long intervals of sun between storms.

FROM BADULLA TO BANDARAWELLA

Tea grows almost out of the rocks on steep hillsides in Sri Lanka. Coolies have had to be tied to tree trunks with ropes to keep them from falling down steep slopes as they work.

A TRANSPLANTED TEA GARDEN

Three-fourths of the world's tea comes from India and Sri Lanka. But it has been tried elsewhere. In the

1930s plant explorer David Fairchild, thinking Americans might be persuaded to take up serious tea drinking, spearheaded an attempt to introduce tea growing in South Carolina with the help of chemist, Dr. Charles Shepard. Fairchild imported the best plants obtainable from the River of the Nine Windings in Eastern China. The Department of Agriculture tried to help Dr. Shepard market his tea, but there was never enough support to mount an adequate advertising campaign. So, although the tea had excellent qualities and had as much alkaloid as Oriental varieties, the South Carolina tea venture failed.

AMATEUR EXPERIMENTERS

Not only distinguished botanists have dreamed of establishing tea in their homelands. Amateurs have leapt to the task. Hotbed for this activity has been British Columbia. In the 1950s a 77-year-old bachelor and prospector with the lovely name of Jervis introduced purple lilac tea to Vancouver.

In 30 years of experimenting, Jervis hadn't found anything that tasted right until he discovered the lilac. It looked like tea, smelled like tea, tasted like real tea.

"Mebbe I shouldn't tell that," he said as he showed off his 60-foot lilac hedge. "Folks will call it scrub tea. It's *not* scrub tea. Scrub tea is always bitter. There's no bitterness in *my* tea."

To defend his tea, Jervis submitted samples to three of Canada's best tea tasters. All seemed satisfied. It tasted a little different, Jervis admitted, but his neighbors liked it well enough.

He harvested only small tender inside leaves, put them to wither for 40 hours, rolled them with a big bottle, withered them again and gave them a second rolling. Then he fired the leaves in his kitchen stove at 250°, sieved the leaves and packed them for sale.

"I'M ONLY REPORTING..."

In northern France, another tea experimenter invented imitation Chinese tea. He browned leaves of a species of birch in a new earthen vessel placed over boiling water. Then he scented them with powdered root of Florence iris. After a few days they were ready. The reporter of the invention declared the brewed tea deceived those who were not in on its secret, adding, "I have not tried it myself!"

DICTIONARY TEAS

Not all teas are Chinese or born of the Queen of Camellias. The definition of tea is wide ranging and includes *any infusion, decoction or extract.*

Four teas have established themselves in the dictionary.

Abyssinian tea is a narcotic, exhilarating tea from leaves of the kat shrub cultivated by the Arabs. Bitter, it is usually sweetened with honey. Chewing the fresh leaves is intoxicating. North Africans include it in their daily diet and buy dried leaves in native markets.

Labrador tea is made from an evergreen shrub of North America. Its narcotic, soothing and stimulating brew comforted early hunters, trappers, miners and explorers in the North. It lends its headiness to Scandinavian beer.

Oswego tea is brewed from fragrant mint that sports a head of bright red flowers. The Indians regarded it as medicine. The Shakers who settled in Oswego, New York, gave it its name. They considered it a tonic.

Hamburger tea is not what you expect. It is a laxative made from senna leaves, manna, coriander and tartaric acid.

SOMETHING MORE THAN WATER

All around the world, peoples have long required their daily beverages to do more than slake thirst.

In South America for rich and poor alike, the beverage is maté. Brewed from leaves of the wild holly of Paraguay and Southern Brazil, the tea is relaxing and stimulating, but intoxicating if drunk to excess. Dubbed *Jesuit's tea* because Jesuits substituted it for brandy, maté derives its name from the Indian word for calabash. Indians made maté in these gourds, tossing hot stones on powdered maté leaves and drinking the resulting tea through a reed. To make maté in a pot, aficionados object, is to spoil its delicate flavor.

The Javanese like tea made from roasted leaves of coffee plants. They much prefer the leaf brew to one infused from the beans. This tea has never become popular with Westerners.

In the Malay Archipelago, tea is provided by a tree of the myrtle family called "tree of long life."

On Mauritius, orchids provide makings of tea.

Texas Indians of the 16th Century made tea from toasted leaves of the yaupon, a species of holly native to Southern United States. This was the "black drink" of the Indians. It contained much caffeine and was a powerful medicine for inducing a state of spiritual presence. Like maté, it was made by boiling leaves in a gourd using heated stones. Then it was poured into a second gourd. White men called it Carolina tea or cassena.

South Africans have a stimulating Hottentot tea and Kaffir tea made from common shrubs containing theine. They also drink *buchu*, a medicinal tea made from aromatic leaves of a heathlike plant.

Natives in the West Indies not only enjoy stimulating teas made with sweetweed shrub leaves. They fatten sacrificial goats with it as well.

TEATOTALING AROUND THE WORLD

All around the world, tea provides a respite from daily chores and cares. Only water outranks it as the world's most popular drink.

Statistically, the English and Irish lead the tea parade, followed by the Americans, Australians, Canadians, Egyptians, French Moroccans, South Africans and Iraqis, to say nothing of Russians. And all these trail the Chinese, greatest tea drinkers of all.

MANY WAYS WITH TEA

When tea was first introduced to Europeans in the early 17th Century, it was mysterious, dear and quite puzzling. Some took tea with salt, ginger and nutmeg. A Jesuit who had enjoyed tea in China added eggs to his tea. Schoolboys spread used leaves on their bread.

A country housewife, thrilled with her first pound of the fashionable stuff, invited neighbors to share it. She boiled it and served it rather like spinach with salt and butter. Her guests detested it.

TEA SOUP

In Tibet and Mongolia, tea cookery has for hundreds of years produced a soup that is both food and drink. Tea leaves are steamed, crushed in a mortar, made into a cake, and boiled with rice, ginger, salt, orange peel, spices, milk and onions. Tibetans consume as many as 30 or 40 portions a day.

In *Lhasa and Its Mysteries*, Col. Waddel described a beverage drunk by the Tibetan all day long:

. . . hot buttered tea, which is really a soup or broth made by boiling tea leaves with rancid butter and balls of dough, and adding a little salt, and straining – a decoction invariably nasty . . . though no doubt wholesome; for it is not merely a stimulating hot drink in the cold, but overcomes the danger of drinking unboiled water in a country where the water supply is dangerously polluted.

PICKLED TEA

In Burma, pickled tea is a delicacy. Tea leaves, mixed and tightly packed with zaungya fruit, are set aside for a week or two. They are dressed with sesame oil and served with powdered dried shrimp, toasted sesame seeds, fried garlic, monkey nuts, sliced coconut and roasted peas.

TEA AU LAIT

In the course of a conference, an Indian businessman has his chaprassi fetch glasses of tea mixed with long-simmered, flavored milk. This is how to make it.

TEA AU LAIT, INDIAN STYLE

1 quart milk
Broken cinnamon stick
Seeds of 4 or 5 cardamon pods
½ teaspoon saffron
1 teaspoon ground almonds
Brown sugar or honey to taste

Combine cinnamon, cardamon, saffron and almond with milk in heavy sauce pan. Simmer for 3 hours, stirring occasionally. Just before removing from stove, add sweetening.

Preheat teapot and pour fresh water at a full boil over 1 teaspoon of good black tea for each cup. Steep 5 minutes.

Add hot milk to tea in a ratio of 1 to 1, or as you like it. Aerate by pouring mixture back and forth between 2 containers 5 or 6 times. Strain and serve.

You can store prepared milk in refrigerator for a few days. Reheat to use.

Finely chopped fresh ginger root added to simmering milk is a good home remedy for sore throat or a cough.

TEA WITH FLOWERS

Teas, made with dried flowers, combine visual drama and aroma as blossoms expand to original size in teacups. In China, the chrysanthemum, plant of immortality, was originally dried only for emperors. Expensive today, it offers a delightful sensation as you watch the large, handsome flower bloom in the cup again. The best grades produce the biggest flowers and cost most.

Linden flowers also add elegance and amber color to tea served in Turkey.

Selma Ekrem recalls harvesting blossoms from a 200-year-old tree at Arnaoutkeuy on the Bosporus. On a beautiful, cool summer day, villagers approached the tree respectfully. They carefully cut flowers close to the stems with scissors and laid them in baskets. They left the topmost flowers untouched to allow the tree to flaunt its crown of blossoms a little longer. They took the cut flowers to an attic balcony and spread the fragrant yield on clean sheets to dry in the sun. When winter came, the dried flowers reappeared, afloat on cups of tea.

TEA IN GLASSES

When Faisal ibn Abdul Aziz ibn Abdul Rahman al-Faisal al-Sau receives at the Royal Palace at Riyadh, one has small glasses of sweet tea in an immense room with a yellow carpet and green walls.

Tea in glasses is traditional throughout the Near East, North Africa and Russia. Moroccans and North Africans like green tea hot, saturated with sugar and flavored with mint. Iranian tea houses serve tea in small glasses with chunks of sugar. No spoon for you, unless you ask, for Persians like to sip tea through sugar lumps.

Istanbul's coffee houses which have been on the scene since the middle of the 16th Century have switched to tea, coffee having become too expensive to import. A shop near the spice market sells a thousand glasses of tea a day.

THE RUSSIAN SOLACE

There are those who say Russia has no tea and that "Russian Tea" is really China tea — the same which reached Europe through Russia by camel train from the early 17th Century on. But the USSR does grow tea, principally in Georgia and Azerbaijan — the farthest north tea is cultivated anywhere.

Russians, of course, have been ardent tea drinkers since 1800. They like tea very hot in glasses with liberal amounts of sugar and lemon.

The reputation of Russian tea is largely sentimental. Smoky Lapsang is the favorite just as it was when pirates prized it as booty. It is usually blended with other teas. Non-Russians either love it or hate it.

A RUSSIAN MUST

Every Russian aspired and aspires to own a samovar. This cherished accessory made its first appearance 200 years ago. A compound word, samovar means "self-boiler" in Russian. Another possible derivation is from the Tatar word, *sanabar*, for tea-urn.

The samovar has a water tank around a central core or miniature stove usually heated with charcoal. The top vent or crown is designed to hold and keep a small teapot warm. Tea infused in the teapot is dark and strong. The idea is to drain as much tea-colored brew from the pot as possible by refilling it again and again from the samovar.

Originally the samovar was equipped with:

Tray big enough to hold accessories
Chimney extension to increase draft of burner
Chimney cap to extinguish the charcoal
Drip bowl
Teapot of the same metal as samovar
Tea glasses with metal holders for the men
Tea cutter for brick tea
Hammer to break rock sugar
Matching jam jar
Tea caddy
Porcelain cups and saucers for the ladies

Samovars were made of tin-lined red copper and brass and ornately decorated silver. They are now made of nickel and chrome. And present-day owners do not confine the samovar to its traditional uses. Prepared punches — hot and cold — and other mixed drinks are just as likely to pour out as hot water for tea.

Russian tea is often laced with fruit brandy or rum. It is proper, also, to bring gifts of Easter cakes for family and friends to enjoy with tea. Tea is served with sweet pretzels and rich cream and it is a welcoming gesture to invite strangers home for tea. Merchants "wet bargains" with tea. Tea goes on picnics. Russians dawdle over tea until it grows cold and still they drink on.

TEA STRAIGHT AND OVER RICE

Tea is as dear to the Japanese. They drink it almost any time. Office workers start the day with a cup. When a guest arrives at home or office, the host routinely serves tea.

No Japanese uses sugar or cream. He wants his tea with its delicate character unalloyed. Sometimes for lunch, he pours very hot tea on rice left over from breakfast and eats it with pickles, broiled salted salmon or salty seafood preserves.

The tea is green. The room where the family has tea is called *Chano-ma*, the tea room. The bowl for serving rice is the *Cha-wan*, tea bowl. In the 16th Century when it became the custom to eat three meals a day, tea bowls were the unit for expressing the quantity of rice. Even today, some call such bowls *Meshi-chawan*, rice-tea bowls.

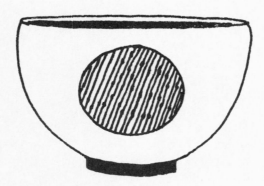

SCOTCH BONANZA

The Scotch excell in teas at which you can expect hot rolls; butter; breads, brown and white; currant bread; girdlecakes; Selkirk bannocks; gingerbread; and apple jelly, all with "an egg to your tea." Scotch tea is so strong, it looks like black coffee.

CANADIAN PREFERENCES

Ever since Hudson's Bay Company introduced tea to Canada in 1715, tea has been the favored drink. Canada not only takes its full share of the world's annual billions of cups, but has preferences by regions.

Maritimers almost match the English in cups per person. Prairie folk like tea the least. In Quebec, the order is, "Make mine green." The most enthusiastic tea drinkers of all are Canadian Eskimos. They like tea strong and very sweet, and they don't mind chewing the leaves.

WALTZING MATILDA

Few are more enthusiastic tea drinkers than the Australians and New Zealanders. Annual per capita consumption is about eight pounds. Blends of India, Ceylon and Java are most popular.

Tea appears seven times a day, beginning before breakfast and ending at bedtime. In between are tea breaks morning and afternoon on the job. Tea is served with milk. The bushman has tea, too, which he makes in a tin billy, often called a "Matilda."

THE WINNERS!

Each year, the English and Irish consume about ten pounds of tea per person. They like blends of India, Ceylon, Java and China teas and also unblended Indias and Ceylons.

In Ireland tea comes to table at breakfast with bacon, sausage, poached eggs, soda bread, butter and marmalade. And at the midnight hour, a tea cart may roll in with homemade fruitcake.

Since half the world's tea exports arrive in the United Kingdom, afternoon tea is an institution not to be trifled with. In England, tea is served in tearooms, tea caravans, tea gardens, restaurants, railway cars, offices and factories. Farmers have their tea fetched to the fields. Dockworkers fought for the right to have an adequate tea and settled the matter with a strike.

Lancashiremen consider coffee "exotic muck" fit for a cold morning if it is spiked with rum. But tea is something else, and it is pronounced "tay" as it was in the days of Swift and Pope. It is drunk at all hours, hot and strong, and with no nonsense about tea bags or lemon. It comes with milk and sugar to taste. If you are attending a wake or it is very, very cold, you may get it with a generous dollop of Scotch.

A WAY OF LIFE

An Englishman's tea is his refuge in times of stress. Gladstone said it all: "If you are cold, tea will warm you — if you are too heated, it will cool you — if you are depressed, it will cheer you — if you are excited, it will calm you."

Construction workers shinny down 20 stories twice a day for tea. Shoppers, male and female, dodge into restaurants, snack bars or hotels for theirs. Bobbies on the beat call a halt for tea.

During World War II, tea was a major morale factor. When workers were asked to work longer hours, Labor Minister Bevin suggested that a factory owner give his men a 15-minute break for tea in the late afternoons. Production increased; so special arrangements were made to supply all factories with tea.

WILL CONTINENTALS JOIN THE TEA SET?

So far tea has failed to cross the Channel. While the average Briton uses tea by the pounds, the average Frenchman cannot be said to drink tea at all. Although tea was very fashionable in France in the 17th Century, annual per capita consumption is measured in ounces today. Frenchmen tend to leave tea drinking to *très snob* little old ladies behind lace curtains.

Italians consume even less. West Germans do a little better, but tend to drink herbal teas.

Only the Dutch approach the English, though they consume a mere pound and a half. Their habit is historical. Ships of the Dutch East India Company carried tea not just for themselves but to supply lucrative smuggling rings plying England's coast.

AND IN THE BEGINNING

The Chinese who started it all are the world's most avid tea drinkers. Everybody drinks tea, no matter what his age, persuasion or the occasion. He drinks tea all day long. He serves it to visitors. He transacts business over tea. His ceremonies progress on tea.

The custom of serving tea to official and private guests is an old one. It is said to have originated with the Sung dynasty when rulers served tea at court on all occasions.

Travelers in China today need never go thirsty. In hotel rooms one finds a small bag of delicious green tea and a big thermos bottle handy with hot water.

Tea houses are everywhere. One generally receives two cups — a big one for brewing and a thimble size one for drinking. The importance of the tea house is reflected in the double meaning of *shang ch'a kuan'r* 上茶馆兒 The phrase means "to go to the tea house," according to Yuen-ren Chao. It also has a special interpretation of "having a dispute arbitrated at a tea house."

CHINA THIRTY YEARS AGO

Our Man pleasantly recalls teas at the Pink House on Waverly Place in Kowloon.

"The Pink House was the bachelor's quarters for captains of the Blue Funnel steamship line famous for capturing the cream of the tea trade. The first time I laid eyes on it, I knew I had come home. Mrs. Mather, the caretaker, reminded me of my favorite aunt, Carrie Crocker. With her delightful English accent she called me 'laddie' and still managed to spare me my dignity.

" 'Rent,' she explained, 'includes a wash amah, a boy to clean your room and make your bed every day, breakfasts every day, tea from 4:00 to 5:00, and dinner six days a week.'

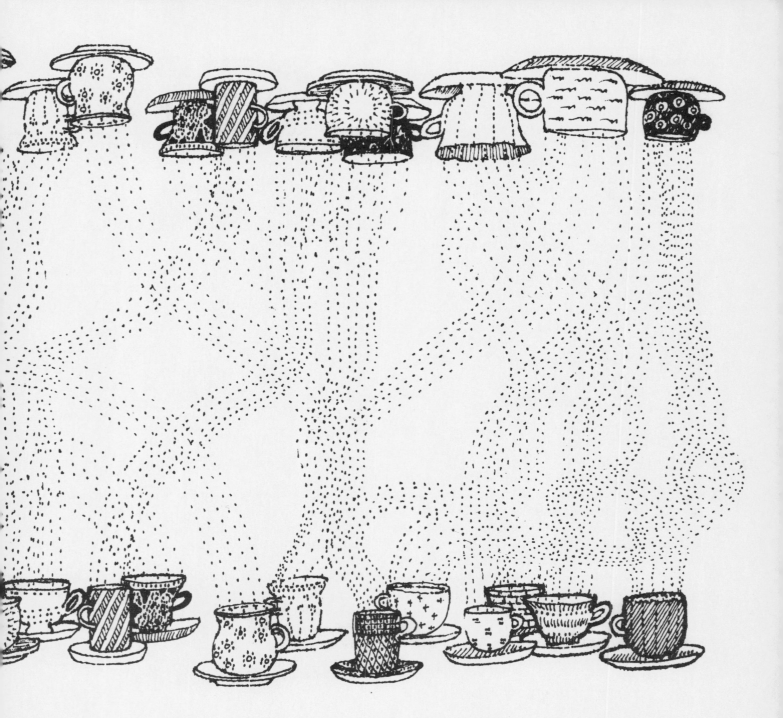

TEA AT THE CRACK OF DAWN

"Promptly as the sun touched the peaks around Hong Kong, the houseboy materialized as if borne on a zephyr. He set a black lacquer tray on a small bedside table with a small cup of steaming tea and a little plate with an unpeeled orange, the blue stencil of the California packer still on it.

"This ritual was frustrating. The tea was too hot. If I drowsed, it became stone cold. If I made a stab at enjoying the luxury in bed, I spilled tea all over. If I peeled the orange, juice dripped on the rug or squirted into my eyes. How, I wondered, did a proper Englishman manage? Here was a rich gift of personal service. I decided to accept the luxurious discomforts of bedside tea as part of my adventure in the Orient.

"Mrs. Mather was utterly dismayed by this ruinous turn of events. It threatened to throw her budget off balance, she protested, and it probably did.

RUINOUS AFTERNOON TEAS

"Afternoon tea was more to my taste. The elegant service and leisurely civility on the veranda in fine weather and in the livingroom when weather was bad agreed with me.

"To this ritual I unwittingly contributed an American revolution. Following a lifetime of profligacy, I innocently spread my bread with both butter and jam. At first my fellow lodgers looked askance. They spread one or the other on their bread, never both!

"Soon they were imitating my extravagance, first to see whether they liked it and then to enjoy the extravagance at dinner.

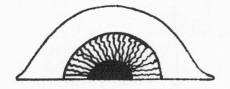

TEA AT THE OFFICE IN HONG KONG

"Many services and ceremonies in my office were delightfully different from anything I had known in California or New York. At intervals all day long, a tea boy made rounds with a teakettle, adding boiling water to tall glasses on every staff member's desk.

"Desks were in closely spaced rows. Two huge fans on tall chrome stands whined away to bring relief from the general heat and humidity. Tea was the only other refreshing amenity and I was amazed how much tea was consumed. There was no tea break. Tea service was simply a fringe benefit and a badge of status — an essential working condition.

ENCHANTED OBSERVER

"Like smoking, sipping tea is a mechanical act, interesting to watch. Glasses were one quarter filled with green leaves. Each had a wooden cover. To sip tea, the drinker grasped the glass with his hand and slipped the cover up and out of the way with two fingers. Refreshed, he slipped the cover back and set the glass down, automatically and without interrupting his work.

"Once I asked a staff member for a sip. He was quick to say, 'You won't like it!' but poured off a small amount. He was right: I did not like it."

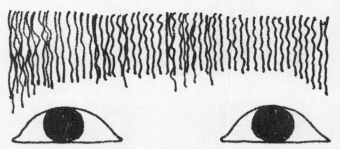

CUSTOMS CHANGE LITTLE

Things are still much the same in Hong Kong. Companies supply tea and a teaboy. There is no formal break for tea or coffee. Because of rising costs of tea, however, the office boy now brews strong tea in a pot and goes around with it in one hand and a kettle of boiling water in the other. First he pours strong tea and then adds boiling water to fill. Plastic has begun to replace tea glass covers of wood and glass. Some tea companies use tea glasses to advertise their tea.

Frieda Chen, a friend from those first days in Hong Kong, tells us, "In our office a couple of glasses from Shanghai have a printed inscription that the glasses are gifts from so-and-so's company. Their glass covers are evidence they are pre-communist issue.

"Habit has a lot to do with tea drinking. We are told that tap water in Hong Kong is drinkable without boiling. During years and years of traveling about China and India, however, we became conditioned to asking for tea because we knew water had to be boiled to make tea. At home, the servant boils and cools water for drinking and stores it in endless bottles.

NO CROWD AROUND THE COOLER

"This is probably why water coolers aren't popular in the Orient. We have a bottle of distilled water on a stand in our office. Few people use it. They still prefer tea or plain boiled water."

TEA AMERICAN STYLE

To use the word "style" with reference to contemporary American tea drinking may be stretching things. Americans consume only a half pound per capita annually. Most of the tea drinkers are in New England and the Middle Atlantic States or have ties to countries where tea drinking is a national pastime.

Tea drinking is seasonal. In the South, little hot tea is consumed in winter, although iced tea is a favorite in summer as it has been since its introduction at the 1904

St. Louis World's Fair. The West and Middle West have little to do with tea.

Most of the tea consumed is a blend of Indias, Ceylons, and Indonesias. It is charged that Americans are indifferent to cup quality and have little knowledge of the types of teas, yet they often carry off the finest teas at auctions.

Americans like their tea to keep pouring during a meal and they prefer to have their croissants, scones and sweet rolls served hot, not cold from a cart as is the British custom.

DRINKING AS DRAMA

The niceties of the Japanese tea ceremony were lost on 19th Century historian Henry James. Its intricacies bored him. His contemporary, Lafcadio Hearn, on the other hand, accepted it as the quintessence of manners. In *Japan: An Attempt at Interpretation*, he wrote:

. . . it requires years of training and practice to graduate in the art . . . Yet the whole of this art, as to detail, signifies no more than the making and serving of a cup of tea. However, it is a real art – a most exquisite art. The actual making of the infusion is a matter of no consequence in itself: the supremely important matter is that the act be performed in the most perfect, most polite, most graceful, most charming manner possible. Everything done – from the kindling of the charcoal fire to the presentation of the tea – must be done according to rules of supreme etiquette: rules requiring natural grace as well as great patience to fully master. Therefore, a training in the tea-ceremonies is still held to be a training in politeness, in self control, in delicacy – a discipline in deportment.

ORIGIN OF TEA CEREMONIES

The Chinese affected ceremonial tea drinking during the Sung dynasty, but let the ritual die.

It was not so for the Japanese. For them the tea ceremony played a special role in life. Artists designed beautiful bowls and jars, teacups, incense burners and utensils for it. Lay people reverenced such tea objects and deeply respected those who created them. The famous Silver Pavilion housed them as treasures. They survive today as the "Higashiyama pieces," jealously guarded and packed off to a safe place in troubled times. Every change of ownership in their long history has been certificated.

AN ARISTOCRATIC PASTIME

An early Japanese captain wrote from a remote province to a friend in the capital, "I have fallen into hell." He felt hopelessly exiled where no one was versed in tea ceremonials. They were indispensable to his happiness, for without them who could discuss aesthetics with him?

Another enthusiast was Yoshimasa, a 15th Century Shogun who became involved out of a desire to escape his strong-willed wife. His inspiration came from the Zen monk, Shuko. Shuko, after 30 years, had laid down rules of restraint and simplicity for tea ceremonies. He and other experts joined Yoshimasa in collecting lavish porcelains and pictures for the Silver Pavilion.

INFLUENCE ON ARCHITECTURE

The Pavilion was a landmark in cultural history. Architecturally, it combined the religious and the domestic and set the pattern for the modern Japanese house. The tokonoma owes its decorative use to the Zen priests and tea masters who used this alcove to display vases of flowers and pictures.

ILL-STARRED MASTER OF TEA CEREMONY

The tea ceremony was perfected in the 16th Century by Sen-Rikyu, a merchant in the port of Sakai. Rare tea objects arrived there from China and encouraged the spread of tea ceremonies.

As tea master, Rikyu was held in such high esteem that even the country's ruler, Hideyoshi, had to humble himself before him. Unfortunately Rikyu coveted personal power. This flaw in character allowed Hideyoshi to trump up a charge that Rikyu had failed properly to judge certain precious tea objects. Hideyoshi ordered him to commit Seppuku.

Rikyu's suicide did nothing to discourage tea ceremonies. Former students promptly set up schools of their own. Tea objects proliferated, as did ways to classify them. The ceremony degenerated into meaningless cant. Rich daimyo competed madly for adjuncts of the ritual. Prices soared. People paid fantastic sums for things simply because they were rare. When Matsunaga Danjo planned to commit suicide, he smashed a precious teakettle to pieces to prevent its falling into the hands of a rival.

PRODIGIOUS TEA PARTIES

Monstrous tea parties took place.

At Kounboum, Tibet, a very rich pilgrim held a tea in a large lamasery. The entire establishment of 4,000 lamas sat in rows to receive two bowls of tea. The host prostrated himself before them until all were served. For his generosity, the great assembly honored him by chanting a psalm.

Hideyoshi also hosted a huge affair. The Midas of his day, he dispensed hospitality grandly and deviously. His celebrated Kitano Tea Party displayed his megalomania.

He announced in Kyoto, Osaka and elsewhere that he would host a great tea ceremony for all — rich vassal and humble peasant alike. Each was to bring his own cup, kettle and mat to sit on. The party lasted 10 days. There were plays, music and dancing. Hideyoshi and other collectors exhibited their art treasurers.

PATTERN FOR EXCELLENCE SET

Despite these latter day excesses, Rikyu had already set the tone, lasting to this day. Tea is still both ritual and refreshment. Many elements affect the tea ceremony — what style of ceremony a host espouses; the time of year; and the occasion. A full scale ceremony may last four hours and include a light lunch and two kinds of tea — a thin brew and a thick green one.

INTRICACIES INVOLVED

Constant elements are harmony, respect, purity and tranquility. Procedures, movements and objects in the room all contribute to the "design." Flower arrangements are natural. Scrolls compliment the season or the occasion. Everything is perfectly balanced.

Talk revolves about the contrived setting. It is good manners to examine the tea bowl and express pleasure in its simple elegance. The eminent authority on Japanese history, Sir George Sansom described the proprieties.

. . . guests discuss gravely the merits of some object of art, perhaps one of the utensils they are using, a bowl of which the glaze harbors rich lights, or an effortless seeming picture on the wall, or a poem or an arrangement of flowers.

A teahouse contains a tearoom and a service room for washing and arranging tea utensils before they are brought into the tearoom. Guests remain in a waiting room until summoned. They enter the tearoom, right foot first, through a low entrance — architecturally designed to require a humble approach.

Guests dress simply. Women wear no perfume or jewelry. All kneel with both knees brought together. This traditional style of sitting arose 300 years ago when many people participated in ceremonies in small rooms. Spacing was critical. This style made room for all.

The tea bowl is of thick pottery, never porcelain. All drink from the one bowl. After studying its beauty, one slowly sips the tea, places the bowl gently on the floor. Special sweets dispel the bitterness of the tea. Guests depart, left foot first.

TO MAKE A GARDEN AND PAINT A PICTURE ARE THE SAME

The teahouse is as complicated as the ceremony. As the ceremony developed into a fine art, it required *chaseki,* a special architecture. This was a modest forest hut with a simple room, unembellished except for a painting, a bit of calligraphy, or a flower arrangement.

With it came the roji, teahouse gardens which led to and around the teahouse, because Rikyu had insisted on a perfect setting for quiet enjoyment of tea. Roji represented lonely paths leading to temples on high ground, their ornamental stone lanterns and water basins meticulously placed.

Roji are now listed as national treasures and pass down as family heirlooms.

BEAUTIFUL PROPORTIONS

It is said Rikyu's ratio was 40 percent beauty and 60 percent practicality. His gardens were simple affairs with simple wickets. Hosts met guests there and proceeded to an inner roji, stopping to rinse their mouths and their hands at a stone basin near the teahouse. The gate was the boundary. It narrowed the view and made the inner garden appear deeper.

Each garden element has a name — stone lamps; inner and outer wickets; water basin; stepping stone nearest the entrance to the teahouse; stone just outside the middle gate where the chief guest meets the host.

SUBTLE COURTESY

While the Chinese left rigid ceremonies behind centuries ago, they observe very special courtesies. They present a cup of tea as a gift, offering it to guests with both hands and with a pleasantry on their lips.

They have their teahouses, too. Their use is informal and devoted to common commerce, refreshment and socializing.

A very famous one — Shanghai's Woo Sing Ding — originally inspired the "Willow Pattern." It was part of a palace complex and garden built in the 16th Century by an ambitious mandarin who sought to rival his emperor Kiei Tsing. His presumption attracted the emperor's extreme displeasure. To save himself, the mandarin quickly offered his palace to the city as a temple. Teahouse and surrounding gardens went public.

Today people approach Woo Sing Ding over its zigzag lucky bridge again. They crowd the place until every chair is taken at small round tables for five, sit on the open porches overlooking the pools and gardens, fan themselves and sip tea as their forebears did 400 years ago.

TEAHOUSE SURVIVES IDEOLOGIES

Old fashioned common sense prevailed recently when the Cantonese custom of enjoying a leisurely pot of tea at the teahouse came under fire.

Masses in Nanhsiung County, Kwangtung, petitioned to have the "Worker-Peasant Soldier Restaurant" restore teatime. A hot discussion ensued. "That would revive one of the decandent 'Four Olds — old customs, old habits, old ideas, and old culture' " someone objected. "Wasn't wiping them out what the revolution was all about?"

They reexamined Chairman Mao's teachings and concluded that teatime was "wrong in form but right in essence;" that it was all right to restore teatime if they distinguished between the new tea breaks and the old bourgeois pastime.

AMERICAN TEAROOMS

It has been said that women occupy half of heaven and half of the teahouses and that tearooms are places where women enjoy everything but tea — sandwiches that don't fill, delicacies that don't nourish and savories that don't satisfy.

This certainly does not apply to tearooms we recall in the Middlewest. They were often genteel old mansions, opened by resourceful widows to the nice people in the community for teas, wedding receptions and other gala family events.

In many ways, they were the best. Women who ran them took pride in impeccable service and shared cooking secrets at their tea tables. The atmosphere was pleasant and in good taste. Food was often superb; deportment, decorous.

As comic Lily Tomlin has said, one didn't go into such places without first blowing one's nose, to avoid being unseemly. And one didn't rummage in her purse for a comb or apply lipstick at table.

MORE THAN SOCIAL GRACE

But times are a-changing. A teahouse on Stanford campus has patrons who don't give a hang for style. They do care about what happens in the world. Their teahouse provides food for the soul, mind and community as well as tea, cookies, steamed sweet buns filled with barbecued pork, wonton with pork, egg rolls and ramen, a tasty Japanese noodle dish. Profits go to community service organizations.

DOWN TO EARTH

All of this is a long, long way from the exotic austerity and dramatic purity of the tea ceremony that elevated the Queen of the Camellias!

The contemporary tea drinker takes a far less esoteric view of his habit than did the ancient Chinese poet who wrote:

The first cup moistens my lips . . .
The second cup breaks my loneliness
The third cup searches my barren entrail
The fourth cup raises a slight perspiration
The fifth cup purifies me
The sixth cup calls me to the realm of the immortals
The seventh . . . I can take no more

Today's tea drinker is relaxed and unpretentious, which is probably as it should be.

TASTING TEA LIKE A PROFESSIONAL

AN ANCIENT TEA TASTING PARTY

Japanese Noh drama includes farcical pieces called Kyogen. One of these, *Shidohogaku, the Horse*, is a hilarious tale of an impoverished noble's scheme to attend a tea tasting.

Having no fine tea to take, he sends his servant to borrow it from a relative and while he is at it to borrow a sword, cloak, horse and groom. The servant hates the job but manages to borrow everything but a groom. The borrowed horse is so high strung, it throws its rider if anyone so much as sneezes.

When the noble presses the servant into the role of groom, he sets the stage for revenge. Knowing he has only to sneeze to unseat his foolish master, the servant determines to do just that.

A PLEASANT PROFESSION

In those times, tea tasting was an amiable social activity like our contemporary wine tasting.

Now tea tasting is a profession. Part artist, part scientist and part businessman, some tasters make a fetish of laboratory impeccability, utter quiet and a pure northlight. Some are institutionalized and perform in groups. Others are famous solo performers. Still others are government agents.

Tea tasters' noses, eyes and sensitive palates dictate the quality of tea drunk every day around the world. They seek bright teas with high grown flavor and point. Brightness sells, they say, because people "drink with their eyes."

HOW TEA IS TASTED

Professionals have their idiosyncrasies. In general, however, a taster brews samples from specific estates. He boils purified water in a stainless steel kettle. It is poured over loose leaves in special lidded bone china cups. These are white to best reveal the color of tea. Teas steep five minutes. The cups are inverted over bowls set before spotless windows. As the tea pours into the bowls, lids catch the leaves for inspection. To check differences in brightness and color from cup to cup, the taster pours a little skimmed milk into each bowl. Taking a spoonful, the taster slurps it in, meditates briefly, then spits the tea out to avoid becoming waterlogged.

AN INDIAN TEA TASTER

In Calcutta, a tea taster may slurp through 120 cups of tea an hour. He wears a long white apron and works in a brightly lit laboratory. He arrives *after* tea has been brewed and cooled. Drinking hot tea, he claims, destroys its true taste.

"I look for the color of the brew before I put a cup to my lips. A muddy color is poor. I like to see a clear, bright shade. The tea should be strong and have the sparkle of champagne."

His brewers follow simple rules:

They boil water only once. Reheated water has an altered taste.

They steep tea exactly five minutes, timing it with a small hourglass filled with pink sand.

On a long counter is a row of white handleless cups. Behind each is a small mug topped with a strainer with a heap of soggy leaves. Tea is brewed individually in these mugs. Behind each mug is a little tin box filled with dry tea leaves.

The taster sucks the tea up forcefully in order to hit the back of his palate. "Number 158, mark good liquor, please," he says to a young man who writes it down. From a tin, he pours dry leaves into a curved piece of cardboard and pours it back into the tin. "Number 156 shows some gold tip (good), too much stalk (bad)." This, too, is recorded.

A junior taster tests along with him but offers no opinions. He may become a full-fledged taster in five or six years. And he may never become one.

AND IN AUCKLAND

A tea taster in Auckland handles 200 pots of tea in a batch. In rows on a bench are gleaming white lidded pots and basins. The amount of tea in each pot is weighed meticulously and steeps for six minutes. A bell rings and a young assistant pours the tea into the basins and tips the tea leaves onto the lid of the pots. The chief tea taster and his first assistant take over.

First they "nose" contents of the pots. They examine leaves for defects of manufacture. They test each yield, then add milk. Both the water and the quality of the milk are important. When Auckland water filters malfunctioned, tasters found it impossible to test accurately.

Tea samples come from commercial houses by air from Calcutta and Colombo. They are tested the minute they arrive. When tasters find the quality they like, they instruct agents to continue buying. If they dislike a tea, they have buyers switch to other tea estates.

Most of the tea for New Zealand comes from Sri Lanka which has 6,000 registered tea gardens. A workbook gives tasters details about each tea estate — its owner, manager, acreage under tea, agents, railheads and other useful data. Dockets accompanying tea shipments are full of information about the tea's manufacture.

A LEGENDARY TEA TASTER

Expert tasters can tell where and at what height a tea grew; whether it was raining at the time of plucking or manufacture; whether it was packed damp; whether it will improve with age; and whether it will marry with other teas.

Such a man 20 years ago was Cecil Browne, one-time tea merchant and official taster for the Canadian Customs and Excise branch of the National Revenue Department. He designed tests to determine whether tea shipped into Canada matched shippers' claims.

Browne's sensitive palate identified hundreds of different teas — where they were grown; their variety; how they were processed; what they should cost and how they should be blended. He "nosed" out quickly whether to reject a shipment just from testing a sample.

THE BROWNE STYLE

Browne used standard equipment. Beyond that, his style was his own.

Three-ounce samples from tea chests in a cargo reached his desk in small round tins. He sprinkled some of the dried leaves on his palm to examine them for foreign matter. Next he weighed out a small quantity from each tin into white bowls and poured boiling water over them. They brewed for five minutes.

Then Browne sniffed the steam rising from the bowls. He sipped each tea slowly, repeating if he doubted his first impression. He made additional tests with wet leaves if he thought he needed further information. Once satisfied, he made a note on a form and allowed a shipment to continue on its way to Canadian consumers or he prevented it from doing so.

A CONNOISSEUR'S BREW

Browne deplored the way tea was spoiled in the making. He thought the use of sugar was a crime, which put him in league with Henry Fielding who said that "love and scandal are the best sweeteners of tea." The only way to drink tea, Browne said, was to drink it clear. Fat in cream completely changes the flavor of tea, he said, and if you must adulterate tea, use plain milk.

This is how Browne made tea at home.

Boil cold water fresh from the tap.

Use an earthenware pot. Heat it first by pouring in hot water and letting it stand for a few minutes.

Toss out the hot water and put in one teaspoon of tea for each serving of two cups.

Pour on freshly-boiled water and allow to infuse for five minutes. If you use a wiry-leafed Orange Pekoe, infuse for 15 minutes.

Do not put pot on direct heat. Keep warm under a tea cozy.

Serve clear.

TEA TASTING AMERICAN STYLE

The U.S. Board of Tea Experts samples tea at the Food and Drug Administration office in Brooklyn. Taxpayers paid $117,250 for this in 1973. The board of seven — a tea examiner and six tea industry experts — meets annually for four days to test, taste and set standards for all tea imported into the United States. Their verdicts may be appealed.

YANKEE INGENUITY

The American tea tasters do what all tea tasters do around the world except that they work as a group, seated around a table with a big Lazy Susan. No walking around a long bench with all the tea bowls in a row! All they do is move the rim of the table and, presto, teas come to the man. The rim accommodates from 20 to 24 samples at a sitting. The center section holds other receptacles and teas being tested.

USING PROFESSIONAL CRITERIA

Can you be a tea taster? Of course! Simply follow the procedures professionals do and look for the same elements that guide all of them: Flavor, fragrance, color of infusion and condition of leaf. Here is a **TEA RATING CHART** to help you describe what taste sensations a tea evokes and sharpen your awareness of leaf qualities and color of infusions. There are easily a hundred special terms in the tea taster's vocabulary. This chart takes note of only the most common.

Tea Rating Chart

CRITERIA	REQUIRED QUALITIES	CHARACTERISTIC DESCRIPTIONS		
Flavor and Fragrance of Infusion	Pungence Point Body	Delicate Mild Subtle Fruity Smoky Cool Intense	Bitter Biting Sturdy Smooth Sweet Brisk	Robust Sharp Winelike Spicy Exotic Refreshing
Color of Infusion	Brightness Clarity	Sparkling Green	Pink Yellow	Amber
Leaf Condition	Purity; absence of foreign objects, stalks, dust and extraneous stuff. Well dried, not blistered or bakey	Clean Aromatic	Fresh Flowerlike	Bold

Well-twisted*
Well-withered**

Open leaves infuse quickly, but well-twisted leaves infuse more slowly and provide a better second cup.

**Brownness and flakiness show poor withering in black teas.*

NOTE: Cost*** provides a final criterion. Next to water, tea is the world's least expensive drink. One pound produces 200 - 240 cups. One pound of coffee in comparison yields only 50 cups.

The price of bulk tea varies from more than a dollar a pound for the least expensive to $12 a pound for extra choice Darjeeling. Many good teas sell for $3 - $8 a pound. Even when you pay $12 a pound, you still manage to brew tea for about five cents a cup. In a word, you can afford the finest teas for almost the same cost per cup as for fine coffees.

***In the summer of 1974.

TEN THOUSAND TEAS

An 8th Century literary man in China poetically numbered teas at ten thousand and a thousand. The Chinese for 10,000 —萬— is the vernacular for something more than mere numbers. It conveys greatness and superiority. Ten thousand and a thousand expresses superexcellence also.

HOW MANY TEAS?

How many teas are there, really? It is difficult to tell how many varieties are produced in China, India, Sri Lanka, Java, Indonesia, Formosa, Africa and South America.

There are three main types — black teas; semi-black oolongs; and green teas. This does not count 1500 or more blends, unnumbered scented blends and a wide range of teas made from exotic flowers and traditional herbs.

To make an educated selection from this incredibly rich store, it helps to know about tea processing, grading and blending.

PROCESSING TEA

The method of processing freshly plucked tea leaves determines types, grades and flavors. Fermentation or the lack of it determines whether a tea is black, green, or semi-black oolong. Leaves for all three may be from the same kind of plant or from the very same plant.

Green tea is not fermented. Black tea is fermented before firing. This frees caffeine from the tannins and develops color and aroma. Oolong tea is fermented briefly before firing.

GREEN TEA

To produce green tea, processors quickly steam fresh leaves. This halts bacterial and enzyme action of fermentation and sterilizes the leaves. Then they machine roll the leaves lightly to give them a curl, break up leaf cells, and free juices and enzymes. All this takes place in an atmosphere carefully checked for temperature and humidity. Finally, leaves are fired or heat dried. This preserves color.

BLACK TEA

Withering

To make black tea, processors first wither freshly picked leaves. They spread the leaves thinly and expose them to sun or artificial heat for 18 to 20 hours until they are pliable. This allows sap and other moisture to evaporate and make the leaf susceptible to a good twist in the rolling process. Successful withering depends on good light, warm temperature and dry atmosphere.

Rolling and Twisting

A roller squeezes tannin and any remaining moisture out of the withered tea. Two surfaces are moved in opposite directions by a crank with eccentric movement This rolls and twists the leaves into mashy lumps. Next a roller-breaker separates the balled leaves and sifts them through a wire mesh.

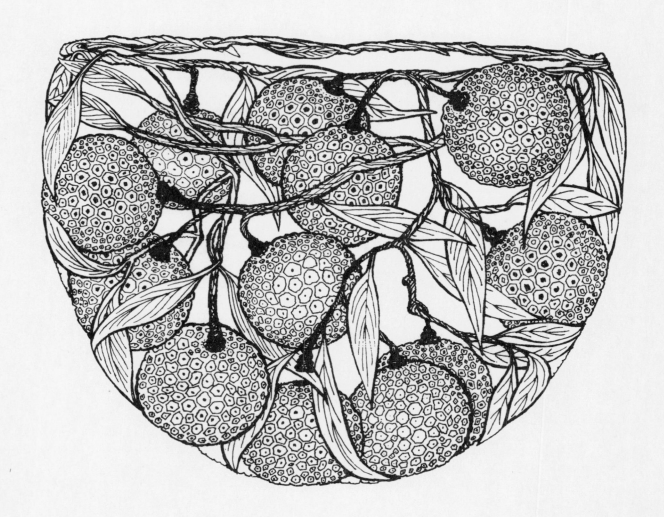

Fermenting

Fermentation follows. Processors spread the leaves on frames and cover them with wet cloths. The leaves absorb oxygen and the resulting chemical change liberates essential oils that give tea its spicy, nutty or flowery aroma.

After fermentation, leaves proceed to a dryer to be fired until absolutely dry, brittle and black. This reduces astringency and sets color and flavor.

Processors need about 4200 pounds of leaves to produce 1000 pounds of finished tea.

GRADING TEAS

Green Tea

Green teas are graded by leaf age and style. In China, major terms in order of increasing size of leaf are *gunpowder,*, *imperial*, *young hyson*, and *hyson*. Hyson was named for an East Indian merchant who first imported this grade of tea. Gunpowder derived its name from its gunpowdery color and pellet-like leaves.

Black Tea

When black teas are dry, they are graded by cutting, sifting and sorting machines. Sifting is accomplished with sieves that oscillate at high speed and eject grades automatically through graded meshes.

Terms used commercially to classify tea leaf size and style vary with country of origin and differ with tea types. The most familiar terms for grades of black tea originated in China where tea is still sifted to produce these grades: *flowery pekoe*, *orange pekoe*, *pekoe*, and *souchong*.

These terms took on different meanings as they were adopted in other countries. For example, finest siftings, smallest leaves and leaf buds of black tea from Sri Lanka and India are known collectively as *pekoes*. Pekoe refers to downiness of young leaves.

The finest pekoes are classified as *broken orange pekoe*; *broken pekoe*; and *broken pekoe-souchong*. *Broken* designates the smallest leaves and pieces. *Orange* refers to the color of the tips. Coarser grades are classified as *orange pekoe*, *pekoe*, and *pekoe-souchong*. Remaining fragments of leaf are rated as *fannings* and finally as *dust*.

Broken orange pekoe is the *crème de la crème*, a fine tea of young golden tips that look like little chips. Too strong for brewing in the teapot, they are added in small amounts to tea blends. To collect them, processors once threw tea against sheets of jute hessian to which the golden tips adhered. In the 1890s, golden tips brought £10 to £35 a pound. A myth developed that the grade name *orange pekoe* was a brand name. Enterprising packers responded by labeling teas "Orange Pekoe" for the market although the term classified only the appearance and size of tea leaves.

BREAKING

Each day's yield of tea goes into graded bins. When there is enough for a "break" — enough to market — 6,000 pounds or more, tea is bulked. The content of a bin of one grade is thoroughly mixed, to assure that any one pound of the tea equals that of any other in flavor and appearance.

SCENTING

Scented teas acquire fragrance from such flowers as jasmine, gardenia, lavender, magnolia and orange. Some are mixed with mint. One method is slowly to dry flowers or leaves in baskets, then reduce them to

powder and mix with tea during final processing.

Another method is to strew handfuls of full-blown blossoms over successive layers of fully fired and still warm tea laid in baskets. The proportion is about three parts by weight of flowers to 100 parts of tea. The final mixture is dried over charcoal for two hours with baskets closed. Flowers are crisp by then and may be sifted out. Tea is then packed.

Tea so scented can be blended with unscented teas in proportion of one part scented to 20 parts unscented.

PACKING

Tea is packed in chests for shipment. Few of us have ever had any experience with teas except those that are in bulk or sealed in bags. Yet for a long, long time they were packed in bricks and tablets. Brick tea was known from the Sung dynasty. It was sent to emperors in golden boxes as tribute. It appeared in Siberia in the 17th Century. When Foochow opened to foreign trade, the Russians began its manufacture there.

Tea bricks were easy to carry by caravan. Stone hard, they served as currency in some districts in old Russia. When tea was carried by railroads and steamships, it maintained its brick form because Asiatics and Europeans recognized it in that form. Hanchow was the chief seat of the industry and imported tea dust and small broken tea from India, Ceylon and Java for the purpose.

BLENDING

Prepared teas from different producers and different areas vary in their constituents — tannins, caffeine, pectins, dextrins, and the essential oil, theol. So, tea wholesalers buy teas from 20 to 30 different areas in order to exploit their distinctive aromas and flavors. Their tea tasters combine and blend teas to produce a uniform quality year after year and, in the process, cater to idiosyncrasies of local tastes. A well-balanced blend may contain some full-flavored teas from Sri Lanka or Darjeeling; some rich, malty teas from Assam, and so on. American blends have much less tannin than English and Australian blends.

Can You Blend Teas Yourself?

Many seem to think that only experts can blend tea successfully or that once they have bought a tea blend, they must not tamper with it.

Samuel H.G. Twining, ninth generation in the famous tea family, champions tea drinkers who want to invent their own blends. He points out that some confirmed tea drinkers are experimenters. "Anyone," Twining says, "can blend his own teas at home very nicely by adding a touch of one or another kind of tea to the basic blend he's used to."

Tea drinking follows moods. You might think Keemun is perfect today and make a simply wonderful tea tomorrow by adding a little Ceylon to it. Some tea retailers will even help you by blending teas to your personal formula at no additional cost if you guarantee to buy a minimum of one pound of your blend.

PACKAGING

Seventy years ago, a thrifty tea wholesaler named Sullivan had the novel idea of sending out tea samples in small, hand-sewn bags of China silk. Recipients quickly discovered they could easily make tea by pouring boiling water over the bags.

In the 1930s, David Coffin, president of Dexter Corporation, observed that tea bags being made of cheese-cloth, gauze and cellophane gave tea a foreign taste. They weren't porous enough and fell apart. They were too expensive. His corporation came out with the thin, long-fiber paper that revolutionized tea bags and tea drinking. Today over half the tea sold in the United States comes in tea bags.

The English shunned tea bags until the late 1960s when their sale expanded. By 1973, they captured about 20 percent of the market. Dexter's tea bag papers now sell in 35 countries around the world. They are catching on in Japan. It has been reported that the Chinese have bought tea bagging equipment to enter the market.

Purists shudder at tea bags. You never get whole, dried tea leaves that way, they say. You pay $3, $4, $5 a pound for tea dust and fannings. A Canadian columnist shuddered to think that tea could cost as much as $100 a pound and more if you buy "those little packages of orange spice tea in bags from the United States!"

You are, in fact, buying convenience when you buy tea bags. Much of the price includes the cost of the packaging. If this doesn't deter you, make certain you buy more tea than bags — no more than 125 tea bags to the pound if you want reasonably full, two-cup tea bags.

Better to Buy Bulk

You enjoy more flavor at less cost when you buy tea in bulk. If convenience is important, use a tea ball. They come in metal at very reasonable prices and in chrome for more. They are large and small and variously shaped. They hold from 1 - 5 and more teaspoons of tea.

THE NAME IS PART OF THE GAME

With characteristic extravagance and imperial exuberance, the Orientals have given their teas such names as would make you want to try a tea just to confirm that it merits its title.

There is *Loong Ching*, Dragon's Well tea from Dragon

Well village deep in the hills behind beautiful Hanchow. Above the village young men tend terraced rows of tea shrubs that yield their famous tea thrice a year. It is light and fresh, smooth and scented.

Cloud Mist green tea descends from the high cliffs of Kiangsi.

Eyelashes of the Swan is available in Singapore.

Iron Kuan Yin, Iron Goddess of Mercy, comes from Fukien, and is so called because its stiff, shiny leaves resist crumbling even after long storage. Bitter and stimulating, it is popular in Southeast China.

Green *Water Nymph* is scented with narcissus and comes from Kwantung, Southern China.

Water Flower green tea is as enticing as its name.

Pearl Dew comes from Japan as does *Genmaicha*, a green tea mixed with roasted unhulled rice.

Other unusual teas are called *Golden Needles*, *Comfort and Peace*, *Blooming Spring* (hyson), *Hard Labor*, *Small Sprouts*, and *White Dawn*.

A WORLD OF TEA TASTING AHEAD

What should you know when you go to buy tea? Names of varieties? Grades and descriptions? Significance of geographical sources? Taste of special blends and types? There is a whole fascinating world of teas to experience and the prospect of years of delicious exploration.

Following is a **TEA TASTER'S GUIDE** to smooth the path. It lists some major varieties, giving descriptions and sources and tasters' definitions and ratings. The Guide gives you space to enter your own reactions so that you can consult them when you shop. The Guide also helps you explore blended teas; flower teas; teas scented with flowers or flavored with spices; and herb teas.

WHAT TO EXPECT

Taste is so subjective that you won't always agree with words experts and tea merchants use to describe the distinctive flavor and aroma of various blends and grades of teas.

There are so many excellent teas that the best way to find out what you like is to taste them. Get a taster's kit from a tea merchant and systematically try them all!

TEA TASTER'S GUIDE

MAJOR TEA VARIETIES	DESCRIPTION AND SOURCES	TASTERS' RATINGS AND COMMENTARIES	YOUR RATING
BLACK TEAS			
Darjeeling	Grown at 7000 ft. in Himalayan foothills; best and most delicate of Indian teas.	Delicate, full-bodied flavor and bouquet; muscatel flavor, dark amber color. Pleasant aftertaste. One cup satisfies.	
Assam	From N.E. India and Pakhistan; grown in relatively low altitudes.	Extra robust, rich, full-bodied, malty taste; cloudy amber color. Lower qualities are bitter.	
Ceylon	Best comes from high districts of Sri Lanka — Uva, Nuwara, Eliji.	Leaves smell of flowers; intense flavor, pleasant aroma and bright color.	
Keemun	From China and Taiwan, the best of China's black teas. Quality varies from year to year.	Thick; superb bouquet; comparable in strength to India black teas. Spicy smoothness lends itself to sugar, lemon or milk. Excellent served with food. Dark amber.	
Lapsang-Souchong	Strong tea from China's Hunan and Fukien Provinces and Taiwan. Often blended with Assam or Ceylon teas.	Strong, hearty; distinctive smoky flavor and aroma. Sweet.	
Chittagong and Sylhet	Pakhistani		
Sumatra	Teas from Sumatra and Java generally used in blends.		

MAJOR TEA VARIETIES	DESCRIPTION AND SOURCES	TASTERS' RATINGS AND COMMENTARIES	YOUR RATING

SEMI BLACK TEAS

Oolong "Black Dragon"	Several kinds come from Amoy, Foochow, Canton in China; Taiwan.	A compromise tea that looks and tastes half of black and half of green tea. Famed for delicacy, bouquet — subtle, fruity taste. Light color.	
Pouchong	Less fermented than oolong. From Foochow and Taiwan.	Often scented with jasmine and gardenia.	

GREEN TEAS

	Grading is often by leaf age and style.	Bitter, they call for short brewing of 1 — 2 minutes — but can be steeped a second and third time.	
Gunpowder	From Taiwan and Anhwei Province, China, tea gets name from gray-green gunpowder color and pelletlike young leaves.	Brews to yellow-green. Pungent, rather bitter.	
Imperial	Balled tea; older leaves.		
Young Hyson	Thin, twisted Chinese tea made from young to medium age leaves.		
Hyson	Hard, twisted leaves. Blueish color.	Fragrant, light, mellow.	
Spider Leg	Japanese tea with long, thin, dark olive twisted leaves. Basket fired.	Delicate and mild; color of pale sherry.	
Gyokuro	"Pearl Dew" — made from best grades; best Japanese tea exported.	Mild, slightly sweet.	
Sencha	Most common commercial Japanese tea; medium price.	Soothing, fresh; served usually to guests with sushi.	

MAJOR TEA VARIETIES	DESCRIPTION AND SOURCES	TASTERS' RATINGS AND COMMENTARIES	YOUR RATING
Matcha	Japanese powdered tea made from young leaves of mature tea plants.	Thick, bitter, frothy; used in tea ceremonies.	
Bancha	Cheapest Japanese tea; has larger, tougher leaves and stems.	Mild; light green color.	
BLENDED TEAS	Teas are blended to suit local preferences, water conditions and to balance pungent, malty types with full-flavored varieties. Some are so common as to have brand names.	Best blended teas acquire their character, aroma, flavor and color from choice of costly teas, some from as many as 30 tea plantations. This insures uniform blend year after year.	
English Breakfast Tea	Term is American and Canadian, not used in England.	Full-bodied black tea with Chinese flavor. Rich, mellow, fragrant.	
Irish Breakfast Tea	Medium strong blend of black teas.		
Russian	Variously named blend of black China teas similar to those brought overland by caravan in early times.	Very strong and dark.	
BLENDED & SCENTED TEAS	Black, oolong and green teas are scented with flowers, herbs, fruit or spices to impart flavor or perfume. Flowers include jasmine, gardenia, orange, lychee. Herbs and spices include ginger, mint, lavendar, nutmeg, cloves and fennel.	All evoke very personal responses. Some make good dessert teas.	
Earl Grey	Blended Indian and Ceylon black teas first created for private use of British noble. Some are scented with bergamot, others with lavendar.	Hearty and aromatic.	

61

MAJOR TEA VARIETIES	DESCRIPTION AND SOURCES	TASTERS' RATINGS AND COMMENTARIES	YOUR RATING
INSTANT TEA	Soluble tea first widely distributed in 1960s and sold in jars or vacuum sealed packets. Made by brewing tea leaves, removing liquid and preserving solids.	Additives may include preservatives and flavorings, mainly sugar and lemon, for iced tea.	
CANNED TEA	Canned iced tea made from instant mix flavored with sugar and lemon; available in fliptop aluminum cans.		
FLOWER TEAS	Blossoms are dried to add visual excitement and aroma to brewing.	These give you the sensation of quaffing a cupful of flowers.	
Camomile		Light apple flavor	
Chrysanthemum	Expensive (as much as $30 a pound), these flowers of immortality were originally dried for Chinese emperors. Best grades have large, handsome flowers.	Slightly bitter-sweet. Some like to add sugar.	
Clover, Red		Delicate flavor; good for daily use.	
Hibiscus		Slightly tart and lemony. Pale ruby color. Good thirst quencher.	
Jasmine		Fragrant, sweet.	
Lavendar		Cooling, delicious, sweet aromatic, exotic flavor.	
Lime		Like camomile, applelike, sweet, aromatic, warming.	

MAJOR TEA VARIETIES	DESCRIPTION AND SOURCES	TASTERS' RATINGS AND COMMENTARIES	YOUR RATING
Linden		Somewhat sweet like jasmine. Amber color.	
Orange Blossoms	Good blended with subtle teas to add zest.	Fragrant, heady, refreshing.	
Rose		Delicate, exotic, fragrant.	
Saffron		Faint curry flavor with pleasant aftertaste; honeyed aroma; clear yellow color; good in daily use.	
Yarrow		Mildly astringent, delicate sagelike taste. Pale yellow color.	

HERB TEAS

DESCRIPTION YOUR RATING

Herb teas are inexpensive, healthful and often delicious, hot or cold. Some have flavor, aroma and appearance equal to that of the best imported teas. Many you can raise in window boxes or pots in your kitchen and use fresh. Flavor of fresh herbs is less concentrated than that of dried herbs and requires greater amounts in making teas. When you use dried leaves, roots or seeds, use 2 teaspoons of herbs to each pint of boiling water or one teaspoon to each cup, depending on potency of herb and your own tastes.

Herbs used singly or in bouquet mixes produce a wide range of distinctive flavors, aromas and pleasant tastes. They also contribute flavor to imported teas, whether hot or cold.

You can buy herbs in health food shops and in the specialty departments of fine stores. Pioneer Americans relied on them heavily as tonics and home cures. Enjoy them for what they are — natural teas, sometimes rich in vitamins — and expect no miracles.

LEAVES
Alfalfa

Rich in vitamins A,D,E, and G. Tea tastes of new mown hay. Often blended with mints.

Angelica	Resembles China tea in flavor.	
Basil	Exquisite aroma. Peppery and clovelike.	
Bay	Pungent, almost bitter. Not a true herb.	
Bee Balm	Another name for it is Oswego Tea. Strong minty taste, aromatic, refreshing.	
Borage	Aromatic, cucumber flavor; cooling; encouraging.	
Catnip	Aromatic, minty.	
Coltsfoot	Fragrant; strong taste; rich in vitamin C.	
Comfrey	Slightly bitter; add lemon balm or apple mint for a milder, sweeter taste.	
Dandelion	Rich in vitamins and minerals; robust, grassy aroma; bland taste, but good blended with mint. Amber color. Good when cold.	
Golden Seal	So grassy, sour and bitter, some like to blend it with mint, thyme, marjoram or black tea. Yellow-green color.	
Hops	Slightly peppery, yet mild. Light yellow color.	
Hyssop	Bitter, minty taste and with slight civet odor.	
Kobucha	Powdered seaweed from Japan.	
Lemon Grass	Best drunk piping hot; lemony, of course.	
Lemon Verbena	Citric fragrance. Delicious added to good black teas.	
Lovage	Distinctive celery flavor.	
Marjoram	Pungent, sagelike flavor; resembles blend of thyme, rosemary and sage.	
Motherwort	Aromatic, bitter taste.	

Nettle	Savory; often added to black teas in ratio of one part nettle to three parts black tea.	
Parsley	Rich in vitamins A,B,C.	
Pennyroyal	Minty, slightly sweet, aromatic. Amber color.	
Peppermint	Good green color and clean mint flavor; delicately fruity. Not as fragrant as spearmint. Used to spice other herbs and teas.	
Raspberry, Red	Astringent and aromatic.	
Rosemary	Piny flavor and incenselike aroma.	
Sage	Heartening, if not too strong a brew. Aromatic, camphorlike; warming, faintly bitter.	
Spearmint	Refreshing. With oregano and thyme makes a bracing breakfast tea and cool afternoon pleasure.	
Strawberry	High in vitamins.	
Thyme	Pungent, spicy; blends well with other herbs.	
Woodruff	Resembles Darjeeling. Mild, sweet, green-yellow tea. Good for daily use.	
Yerba Buena	Indescribable fragrance.	
Yerba Maté	Refreshing; contains caffeine and tannin; stimulating and nourishing. Grassy taste.	
Yerba Santa	Clear champagne colored tea with dry, clean cinnamic fragrance. Pleasant peppery aftertaste.	

ROOTS

To make tea, boil 15 — 20 minutes and strain.

Chicory	Coffeelike, slightly bitter; without caffeine.	

Comfrey	Somewhat astringent; source of vitamin B12. Unusual, good flavor.	
Dandelion	Makes coffeelike tea, bitter but warming.	
Ginger	Hot, spicy, warm aftertaste; a comfort when you have a cold.	
Ginseng	Dried roots imported from Orient. Parsniplike, it is sold in Chinese herb shops as a general tonic for a long list of ills. So bland, it is improved by adding sugar or honey. Very expensive — $130 for a pound of redroot; more than $1200 for whiteroot, which is packaged in gold foil and handled like a jewel.	
Licorice	Like anise — sweet; satisfying thirst quencher.	
Marshmallow	Soothing.	
Sarsaparilla	Tonic and sharp.	
Valerian	Soothing, strongly scented, sleep inducing.	

SEEDS & BERRIES

To make tea, bruise seeds slightly in mortar to bring out oils. Simmer 5 — 10 minutes. Strain and serve piping hot.

Anise	Aromatic and sweet.	
Celery	Aromatic, pungent, sweet and nutty tasting.	
Fennel	Aromatic and spicy like nutmeg.	
Foenugreek	Delightfully aromatic, carmellike, sweet. Seeds used to make artificial maple flavoring.	
Senna	Almost tasteless; often brewed with coriander seeds for more pungent taste and aroma.	
Juniper	Piny tang, bittersweet, fragrant and spicy.	
Rose Hips	Fruity, beautiful orange brew, high in vitamin C.	

TIPS ON BREWING & STORING

Complaints that few housewives brew good tea are hoary with age. All of 1200 years ago, Chinese poet Li Chih Lai grumbled that one of the most deplorable things in the world was the waste of good tea in its brewing.

With authoritarian advice coming at her from artists, emperors and others of that ilk, it's a wonder the homemaker brewed any tea at all. Lo-yo advised her to brew tea from leaves picked during certain moons under clear skies.

A Chinese emperor, obviously with the master's touch, suggested, "Set an old three-legged teapot over a slow fire. Fill it with melted snow. Boil for as many minutes as it takes to turn crayfish red. Pour the boiling water over the tea leaves and let it remain until the vapour melts into a thin mist which floats upon the surface." That done, you could drink the precious stuff at leisure and drive away the five causes of sorrow.

In the opening years of this century, Okakura Kakuzo was scaring us all by flatly stating that "Tea is a work of art and needs a master hand to bring out its noblest qualities."

EVEN YOU AND I CAN DO IT!

The tea brewer now has advice that, thankfully, brings tea down to earth for us all.

Even the experts' tea is not always accepted by confirmed tea drinkers. Consider the flap surrounding the British Standards Institute's proposal for professional tea tasters who wanted to brew a good cup of tea and select and blend teas successfully.

BSI recommended designs for appropriate pots and prescribed suitable water, length of infusion, amount of tea to use, when to add milk and such relevancies.

Use a white porcelain or glazed earthenware teapot, BSI ruled, with a loosely fitted lid. Put in tea with a weight of two percent of the mass of water. Keep the level of water in the pot within four millimeters of the brim.

The Institute hedged when asked whether the pot should be warmed first and whether milk should be poured into a teacup before or after tea is poured.

MILK IN YOUR TEA?

Unless it is contrary to normal practice, said the Institute in a mood to equivocate, pour milk into the cup first. But if you like to add milk afterwards, "experience has shown that best results are obtained if the temperature of the tea is in the range of 65° — 80° C. when milk is added."

TEA DRINKERS, ARISE!

A London housewife took BSI on. "My mother told me always to warm the pot with boiling water before making tea in it. That is what I do!"

Another protested, "How can BSI fail to mention the need for warming the pot? That's crucial. It's the only thing that really counts. As for the rest of it, it sounds as if they are talking about a laboratory, not a kitchen."

"Who knows what a millimeter is anyway," scoffed still another. "As for that technical nonsense about the tea being two percent of the mass of water, what's wrong with the old faithful one spoon for each cup and one for the pot? It was good enough for my old grannie and it's good enough for me."

CANADIAN GUIDELINES

Canadians roared, too. "That's not our tea," they said. "Bloody ridiculous! Tea making is intuitive. You can't legislate it. You don't make tea with a slide rule." So the Canadian Tea Council suggested four, easy, all-inclusive steps to make perfect tea.

1. Warm the teapot with hot water; then throw out the water.
2. Use one tea bag for two cups; or one teaspoon of loose tea for each cup plus one for the pot; or one level teaspoon for each cup of instant tea in the cup or pot.

3. Add fresh bubbly boiling water. (Rising steam does not mean water is at a bubbling boil. Do not use hot tap water: it will ruin tea.)
4. Brew five minutes.

IMPORTANT EXCEPTIONS

A prestigious tea man came forward in Vancouver to caution, "Brewing time depends entirely on the tea. A Darjeeling may take seven or eight minutes; a Ceylon, only three or four. A China tea can be served almost immediately."

UNITED STATES TEA EXPERTS

The U.S. Board of Tea Experts suggested these rules:

1. Use a tea pot. It holds temperature at a very high level. Don't steep tea in a cup. It lets the best flavors and aromas escape.

2. Use one teaspoon of tea or one tea bag (plus one for the pot) for each cup.

3. Use fresh, furiously boiling water on tea leaves. This releases full flavor.

4. Use a clock when brewing tea. Take no less than three nor more than five minutes.

A FULL ROLLING BOIL IS IMPORTANT

Mimie Ouei in *Art of Chinese Cooking* points to an easily verifiable fact. If tea water you use has not reached a rolling boil, half the leaves in the pot will float and remain so during the brewing. Most of the rest of the leaves will stay on the bottom.

With freshly boiled water, two-thirds of the leaves will float at the start of brewing, tea leaves on the bottom will rise and some on top will fall. In five minutes, all leaves will be on the bottom and you will have a tea with good body and flavor.

Also, if tea water is allowed to continue boiling furiously, the action drives oxygen out of the water and tea made from it will taste flat.

A MATTER OF PERSONAL PREFERENCES

"Every man to his own taste," said the old man as he kissed the cow. And so it is with tea. Some like it weak. Some like it strong. Others want sugar and milk. Still others ornament tea with condiments and slices of fruit and jam.

"The right way," said Gervas Huxley, tea connoisseur, "is the way *you* like it best." The only other safe thing that can be said is that tea itself has some small requirements, if you want to make the best of it.

THE POT

Make Tea in a Teapot. This is a good excuse to have fun selecting a pot, finding a jewel that embellishes your life and is even worth mentioning in your will.

Coming from a region where teas were remote events in high society, I early regarded tea as exotic and teapots as something to aspire to. My first was more a possession than a utensil. It was small, beanpot brown and English. It poured like a dream. It was a sad day when it was broken.

Over the years we progressed to pots commissioned from fine potters, to Wedgwood creamware, to rich silver, to porcelain in a Chinese basket cozy.

The best of the pots hold heat without heating up the handles. A little sterling pot has small ivory rings cutting through the handle, top and bottom, to keep the metal from heating up. This design is something to think about if you are buying metal.

Teapots should be big enough to serve all the guests. They should be well balanced and not easy to tip. A pot in our collection is stoneware. Beautiful as it is, I would think twice before having another. It is simply too heavy, filled or unfilled, and serving tea ought not require you to be a weight lifter.

The lid on a pot is important. Make sure it is loosely fitted, has a hole in it, and doesn't fall off when you pour. The spout, too, is a consideration. If it is too low, water will pour out even when water is low in the pot. It should pour smoothly. And check to see whether the spout drips. Finally, the pot should be easy to clean.

When you have found a pot you think is beautiful, sit down with it, handle it, ask to see how it pours with water in it. Grasp the knob of the lid. Is it easy to do? Is the handle easy to manipulate or will it interfere with removing the lid, filling the pot, rinsing and cleaning? Now, you are ready to buy!

THE WATER

Use furiously boiling water. Warm the pot by filling it with boiling water before steeping begins. Empty it. The water to be poured over the leaves for brewing should be freshly drawn and just brought to a full boil, no more.

THE TEA

To the heated pot, add one teaspoon of tea for each cup, more if you like it strong. If you like your tea weak, make it full strength; **then** add hot water to your cup after you pour the tea. This assures good flavor and aroma.

STEEPING

After pouring boiling water over tea leaves, put lid on at once and cover with cozy. Steep five minutes.

TEA OR MILK FIRST?

Even a queen may err. Buckingham Palace sources say Queen Elizabeth pours tea first, then adds milk — an error according to the British Standards Institute. Milk comes first; otherwise, it is scalded and this affects taste. Samuel Twining agreed but for a different reason. Putting milk into an empty cup — especially one of fine china — protects it from cracking or breaking when hot tea is poured into it.

TEA STORAGE

Because tea is delicate and absorbs flavors and moisture, airtight containers are necessary to preserve it. Its life and fragrance are said to fade after six months on the shelf, but we have found little deterioration in teas kept in good caddies for two years or more.

Like teapots, tea caddies are among the most interesting appurtenances to collect. We have an old cylindrical Korean tea caddy that has a sleeve closure. Plain tin inside, it has an exterior subtly decorated in red, gold and black floral arrangements.

The earliest caddies Europeans saw were Chinese porcelain, often blue and white and shaped like ginger jars. Lids and stoppers were china.

At first, the English imitated them. Then they created their own forms. Ceramic factories vied with each other in supplying the fashionable containers.

Tea caddies were made in a variety of shapes and from wood, pewter, tortoiseshell, brass, copper and silver. Most commonly they were of wood. Many Georgian box-shaped caddies survive in mahogany, rosewood and satinwood, often mounted with brass and delicately inlaid with knobs of ivory, ebony or silver. The Dutch made them in earthenware Delft, the best of theirs enamelled and enriched with ciphers and heraldry.

A NO-NO CADDY

Wooden caddies with lid and lock had several inner containers to hold tea and sugar. Locks kept servants from taking a clandestine nip when tea was very expensive. When tea became common and housewives no longer found it urgent to secure it, the locked tea caddy fell into disuse.

72

CUSTOMS, CIVILITIES & COLLATIONS

A TOUCH OF CLASS

Their Lordships Ossory and Arlington gave tea social prestige when they brought it to London from Holland in 1666.

Country houses in their day provided prodigious breakfasts with joints of beef on the sideboard. Sportsmen drank ale, scorning such "slops as tea." And they went hungry until dinnertime about 8:00 p.m. Lunch as a set meal did not exist.

Anna, wife of the seventh Duke of Bedford, to put a stop to this punishing routine, introduced tea at 5:00 in her rooms. This humane custom originated at Belvoir Castle where the duchess often visited. Although tea was expensive, she happily shared the luxury with other ladies staying at the castle and served it with cakes. She continued the practice when she returned to town and sent cards to friends promising "tea and a walk in the fields." By degrees, afternoon teas became the fashion.

TIME TO FEED BODY AND SOUL

From early times, tea was a family beverage that men and women could share and enjoy together in an extended social setting. Today, teatime may begin as early as 3:00 and end as late as 7:00. For many around the world, the custom is assurance of family continuity and tranquility. It is a time for happy confidences, inspired talk and small gossip. Invited guests come to taste precious homemade things the hostess invents or makes from heirloom recipes.

Certain recipes turn up at teas again and again with different names. One of these is for Gold Nuggets. They are so good they melt in your mouth.

GOLD NUGGETS

- 1 cup butter
- 6 heaping tablespoons powdered sugar
- 2 cups cake flour
- 1 teaspoon vanilla
- 1 cup finely chopped walnuts

Allow butter to reach room temperature. Cream well with sugar. Add flour, vanilla and nuts. Roll into walnut size balls and bake on unbuttered sheet at 350° for about 12 minutes. Cool on rack and dust with powdered sugar.

Yield: 50 nuggets

A FEATHER BOA KIND OF COOKIE

Niel Gehrke's Jam Bars are two-layer confections that will invest your tea table with frilly extravagance. They are fun to put together.

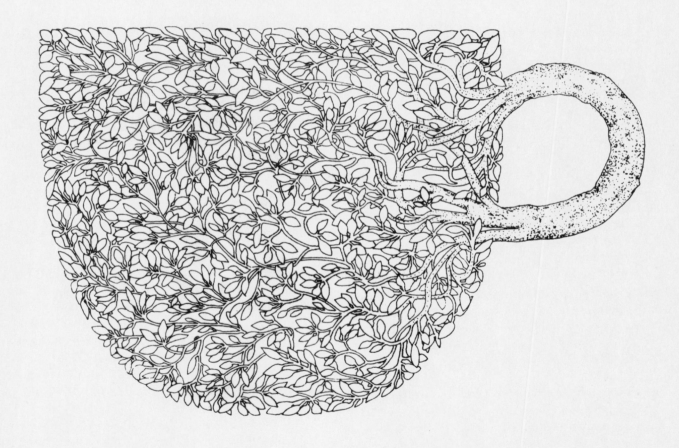

74

JAM BARS

½ cup sugar
1 cup all purpose flour
1 teaspoon baking powder
¼ teaspoon salt
¼ teaspoon grated orange rind
1 egg
¼ cup soft butter

Sift together sugar, flour, baking powder and salt. Add orange rind, egg and butter. Mix well. Press into 8" square pan. Bake 10 minutes at 350°. Remove from oven and spread with ⅓ cup strawberry jam.

Spread with meringue prepared as follows:

1 egg
½ cup sugar
¼ cup soft butter
¾ cup coconut

Beat egg well. Add sugar and beat until thick. Beat in butter and add coconut. Spread over jam and return to oven. Bake at 350° for 25 minutes. Cool in pan and cut into narrow bars.

Yield: 3 dozen

EASY TO MAKE, NERVE WRACKING TO BAKE!

Here are very fragile, crisp and chewy wafers that are worth any battle you have getting them off the baking sheet!

WALNUT WAFERS

1 egg thoroughly beaten
1 cup brown sugar
3 tablespoons flour
Pinch of salt
1 cup broken walnuts

Beat egg, add sugar and mix well. Add flour and salt. Stir in walnuts. Drop by teaspoon on buttered sheet and bake in 325° oven for 5 - 7 minutes. These burn easily; so keep an eye on them. Remove from sheet while still warm.

Yield: 3 dozen

A CENTENNIAL TEA

Last year on Prince Edward Island, Canada, a 4-H Club explored kitchen practices of a hundred years ago. They gathered recipes from parents, grandparents and elderly residents in the process.

The Lieutenant-Governor and his Lady capped the project with a Centennial Tea. Dainties prepared for the event from 100-year-old recipes included Scripture Cake, Gingersnaps, and Thimble Cookies.

FOLLOW THIS RECIPE RELIGIOUSLY!

Originators of Scripture Cake posed the recipe as a guessing game at sewing bees and quilting parties to test guests' knowledge as Bible students and their ability as cooks. This activity discouraged idle gossip at gatherings.

The cake improves in taste if allowed to stand for 24 hours after baking. Have someone you love around to share the beautiful, carmelly dough. The finished cake is delicious, moist and wholesome and freezes well.

SCRIPTURE CAKE

Judges 5:25
Jeremiah 6:20
Isaiah 10:14
1 Samuel 30:12
Genesis 43:11
1 Kings 10:10
Exodus 16:31
Genesis 24:17
1 Kings 4:22
Leviticus 2:13
Amos 4:5

Follow Solomon's advice for making good boys (Proverbs 23:14, "beat him with a rod") and you will have a good cake. Amen.

This translates very loosely into the following, although the order of listing is not identical to the Scriptural quotations nor is there any quotation that mentions almonds. As you might guess there are other recipes for Scripture Cake. A New England version cites Nahum, Numbers and Chronicles. Have fun checking them out!

TRANSLATION

1 cup butter
3 cups brown sugar
6 eggs
¼ cup honey
¾ cup water
3½ cups whole wheat flour
⅛ teaspoon salt
4 teaspoons baking powder
¼ teaspoon each: cloves, cinnamon, nutmeg, mace
⅛ teaspoon allspice
2 cups raisins, chopped
2 cups chopped Smyrna figs
1 cup chopped almonds

The easiest way to make this big cake is to cream softened butter and sugar with an electric mixer. Add eggs, one by one; then honey and water.

In a separate bowl place all dry ingredients and stir until thoroughly blended. Stir in chopped fruit and nuts and finally the butter-sugar mix. Beat well and pour into buttered, lightly floured oblong pan 9x13x2½. Bake at 325° for 1½ hours. Start checking, however, when cake has been baking for an hour.

This cake is big enough for a collation. Serves 30 to 40.

A SHOW-OFF COOKIE

Thimble Cookies are very handsome little confections with their bristling coats of nuts and colorful jam caps. They look so elegant that you'd never dream an amateur could make them so easily. We chopped nuts with our lightest Chinese cleaver and made quick work of the hardest part of preparation. We used leftover filling from Eccles Buns and found its strong lemon and citron taste perfect to make these very piquant tidbits. (See Page 84 for recipe.) You can use various colored jams to make your cookie display sparkle.

THIMBLE COOKIES

½ cup softened butter
⅓ cup sugar
1 egg yolk
½ teaspoon vanilla
1 cup whole wheat flour
1 egg white lightly beaten
1 cup finely chopped walnuts
Your favorite jam or filling

Cream butter and sugar until light. Blend in yolk and vanilla. Stir in flour. Chill until firm. Roll dough into small balls. Dip each in egg white and roll in chopped nuts. Put on lightly buttered sheets. Press finger into center of each ball to make a slight depression. Bake at 350° for 5 minutes, press spoon into each depression and continue baking 8 - 10

minutes until set. Cool on rack and fill indentations with jam when ready to serve. Cookies freeze beautifully.

Yields: 40 cookies

WHOLESOME AND SNAPPY

We don't ever recall making gingersnaps quite like these. Boiling molasses and butter together and adding soda in hot water brings a color experience that is one of the joys of being a cook. The bubbly liquid is a brown gold of exciting richness.

The finished cookie is as crisp as you could wish. Because we didn't want to save the scraps and bunch them together for re-rolling with the rolling pin, we made little balls the size of a walnut and rolled them in sugar to make a distinctly different cookie — plump, cracked on top, crisp on the outside and soft on the inside — at least the first day! You wouldn't believe they came from the same dough or the same recipe.

GINGERSNAPS

1 cup molasses
½ cup butter
1 teaspoon soda
1 tablespoon boiling water
2½ cups flour
½ teaspoon salt
1½ teaspoons ginger
½ teaspoon cinnamon
Sugar for sprinkling

Bring molasses and butter to boil in sauce pan. Cool. Add soda mixed with boiling water to molasses mixture and stir.

Sift 2 cups of flour with salt and spices into mixing bowl. Stir in molasses mixture. Add remaining flour to make an easy-to-roll dough. Chill. Roll dough very thin on a lightly floured board. Sprinkle with sugar and cut with 2-inch round cookie cutter. Bake on ungreased cookie sheets at 375° about 5 minutes or until set.

Yield: 7 dozen

TEA DOWN AN ENGLISH LANE

Tea in an English home is laid on the diningroom table on an embroidered tea cloth. There is a strict order of eating — first savory, thinly sliced sandwiches with cucumbers and tomatoes and watercress from the kitchen garden. Then you have finely sliced buttered bread spread with homemade raspberry jam. After that, you have a choice, perhaps, of a gingerbread square, shortbread, parkin, a slice of chocolate layer cake, or a piece of rich Dundee fruitcake.

Children have milk and grownups drink tea. If men folk arrive at the end of the tea hour, about 5:30, they have tea and a slice of Dundee cake.

Here are some recipes for duplicating such a tea.

CUCUMBER SANDWICHES

1. Arrange thin slices of peeled cucumber on buttered white bread and sprinkle with dill. Top with second slice of bread.

2. Place thin slices of cucumber and leaves of watercress on buttered whole wheat bread.

3. Place paper-thin slices of cucumber on rounds of white bread cut to match and spread with butter mixed with minced parsley, smoked salmon and lemon juice.

RASPBERRY JAM

6 cups raspberries well packed
4 cups sugar
⅓ cup lemon juice

Combine berries and sugar in kettle. Let stand until sugar dissolves, stirring often. Place over high heat and bring to rapid boil. Boil 5 minutes, timing from the minute mixture breaks into rolling boil. Add lemon juice and boil 5 minutes more. Pour into sterile glasses and seal with wax.

Yields: Six 8-oz. glasses

AN ANCIENT SWEET

Gingerbread was known in England before the Norman Conquest, and ginger, next to pepper, was the most valued spice in the 13th and 14th Centuries. Very early cookbooks mention it variously as *Gensbread*, *Gengerbread*, and *Gynger breed*. Cooks often used wooden molds to shape gingerbreads like men and animals.

Poet Cowper loved having gingerbread with his tea and often enjoyed it along with "toast made fresh." Elizabeth Goward of Victoria adds lemon peel left over from fish night and soaked and cooked with sugar. We have used her idea in the following recipe. The resulting gingerbread is deliciously soft inside and has a crusty outside. We used the chopped peel of one lemon (which boils down to ½ cup) and cooked it in 1 cup of water. When the peel was soft, we pressed out the liquid and used it, boiling hot, on the shortening, adding hot water needed to fill ½ cup.

GINGERBREAD WITH LEMON PEEL

½ cup cooked lemon peel
½ cup boiling water
½ cup shortening
½ cup brown sugar
½ cup molasses
1 beaten egg
1½ cups flour sifted with
½ teaspoon salt
½ teaspoon baking powder
½ teaspoon soda
¾ teaspoon ginger
¾ teaspoon cinnamon

Pour boiling water over shortening and add remaining ingredients. Beat until smooth. Bake in buttered pan 8" square in moderate oven for 35 minutes. Cool in pan.

Yield: 9 servings

THE PROTEAN SCOTCH

The Scotch are famous for their small cakes and have many recipes for shortbread. Recipes differ from area to area. The shortbread is especially associated with New Year's Eve. Here are two versions. The basic recipe is easiest accomplished with an electric mixer. The sherry version is much easier to handle and provides great fun for the cook who wants to experiment with different shapes.

BASIC SHORTBREAD

1¾ cups flour
¼ cup rice flour
⅔ cup soft butter
⅓ cup sugar

Cream butter until soft. Gradually add sugar, then sifted flours until you have a crumbly mix. Now get your bare hands into the dough and work it until you have a stiff paste. Roll out ½ inch thick and cut into

fancy shapes or press into a shortbread mold. You can also roll out thin and stamp into small rounds or cut into strips and prick with fork. Place on unbuttered sheet and bake at 300° until nicely brown.   Yield: 4 dozen +

SHERRY SHORTBREAD

1 cup soft butter
¾ cup sugar
½ teaspoon almond extract
1 teaspoon grated lemon rind
1 egg well beaten
3 cups all purpose flour
½ teaspoon baking powder
1 teaspoon salt
¼ cup sherry

Cream butter, sugar, almond extract and rind until fluffy. Beat in egg and add flour sifted with baking powder and salt, alternately with sherry. Chill dough thoroughly, over night if you like. Roll out small portions at a time on lightly floured board. Cut with different shaped cutters or press with molds. Bake on unbuttered sheet at 350° until light brown, about 8 minutes.   Yield: 5 dozen+

CAKES THAT ORNAMENT THE TEA TABLE

Here are recipes for a good, moist fudge cake and a traditional Scottish fruitcake.

CHOCOLATE LAYER CAKE

½ cup grated chocolate
½ cup milk
½ cup brown sugar

1 cup brown sugar
½ cup butter
2 beaten eggs
⅔ cup milk
1 teaspoon vanilla
2 cups flour
1 heaping teaspoon baking powder

Boil together first three ingredients until creamy. Cool.

Combine 1 cup brown sugar, butter, eggs, milk and vanilla. Mix well and beat in boiled mixture. Add flour sifted with baking powder. Bake in two buttered layer pans at 350° for 25 minutes. Cool completely on wire rack before frosting.

FILLING AND FROSTING

1 cup chocolate chips
1 cup powdered sugar
2 tablespoons butter
1 egg yolk
1 teaspoon vanilla
Enough light cream to mix

Heat all in double boiler until smooth. Cool a bit and apply to lower layer. Put top layer on and finish frosting the cake.

Dundee cake, like shortbread, appears in many variations from simple to lavish. It takes its name from Dundee, a Scotch seaport celebrated for its confections and marmalade. A fruitcake, it is sometimes made with orange juice and topped with slivered almonds and candied fruit.

DUNDEE CAKE

¾ cup butter
½ cup sugar
½ cup corn syrup
1 teaspoon vanilla
3 eggs
1 tablespoon grated orange rind
1 cup chopped raisins
½ cup currants washed and dried
½ cup chopped citron

2 cups sifted cake flour
½ teaspoon baking powder

Cream butter with sugar, syrup and vanilla until light. Add well beaten eggs and rind. Add fruit and blend lightly. Add sifted dry ingredients gradually. Pour batter into buttered tube pan or round torte pan (9x3 inches) lined with heavy brown paper. Bake at 325° until golden brown, about 1½ hours. Cool in pan for 15 minutes before removing and placing on rack. Cool thoroughly before serving. Some let cake stand a week before cutting. Store in breadbox.   Yield: one 2-pound cake

THE GINGERBREAD COOKIE

This big North Country cookie is made with syrup or molasses and oatmeal. There are a number of recipes for it. Here is one.

PARKIN

2 tablespoons chilled butter cut in ¼-inch cubes
½ cup all purpose flour sifted with
    ½ teaspoon soda
    ¼ teaspoon each of ginger and cinnamon
¼ cup brown sugar
¼ cup regular oatmeal
3 tablespoons golden syrup or molasses
1 egg lightly beaten
Blanched almonds split in half

Chill mixing bowl. Combine flour sifted with soda and spices with sugar and oatmeal. Stir well. Add chilled butter and rub into dry ingredients until it looks like coarse meal. Warm syrup so that it runs freely, cool a bit and beat in egg. Pour over flour mix and beat to a paste. Drop by tablespoon on well buttered sheet, two inches apart. Put an almond on top of each and bake at 275° until done. Cool on rack.

Yield: 12 big cookies

AN ALL-TIME FAVORITE

God must love scones because there are so many of them. They are made plain with white flour. They are made fancy with currants or sultanas. They are made with whole wheat. They are made with soda and sour milk or buttermilk. Some are round and some are triangular or square. So invent your own!

They require only a small amount of shortening, want rapid mixing to a soft dough, light handling, and baking in a quick oven to avoid the escape of the gas through the dough.

CREAM SCONES

2 cups flour sifted with
   3 teaspoons baking powder
   ½ teaspoon salt
   2 tablespoons sugar
¼ cup butter
½ cup cream
2 beaten eggs

Cut butter into sifted dry ingredients. Combine eggs and cream and add. Pat to ¾ inch thick. Cut in squares or triangles, sprinkle with sugar and bake at 375° until lightly brown, about 20 minutes. Serve hot with strawberry jam.

Yield: 1 dozen

SOME LOVELY STUFF

One of the most versatile of quick breads is the Irish soda bread. Since I am part Irish myself, I hope the Irish will forgive me for saying that I have made it a hundred ways and they all turned out beautiful. We can't say which number this is. It is very homely and satisfying with sweet butter and a mild cheese, perfect for late afternoon tea with little else.

SODA BREAD WITH ROSEMARY

⅔ cup whole wheat flour
⅓ cup soy flour
1 cup unbleached white flour
2 rounded tablespoons sugar
½ teaspoon salt
1½ teaspoons baking powder
½ teaspoon soda
1 teaspoon powdered rosemary
¼ cup sunflower seeds
1 egg lightly beaten
½ to ⅔ cup buttermilk
1 tablespoon melted butter

Sift flours and dry ingredients together into a bowl. Add sunflower seeds. Beat egg lightly in separate bowl, add buttermilk and butter. Stir into dry ingredients until moistened throughout. Knead lightly right in the bowl. Form a ball and flatten it slightly. Cut a cross on top of the loaf to scare off the devil, place on buttered pan and bake at 350° for 30 – 40 minutes until golden brown. Cool slightly and serve thin slices.   Yield: 1 loaf

PUFF PASTRY EVEN YOU AND I CAN MAKE!

One of the delights of travel has been the chance to roam through bakeries and buy things that look interesting. We first found Eccles Buns in Vancouver. Shaped like turnovers and glistening, they did not even have a name until we asked the clerk. A foods dictionary describes them as round puff pastry filled with brown sugar, currants and spices. This is how you can make them for tea.

ECCLES BUNS

PUFF PASTRY, SIMPLIFIED

½ cup milk
2 teaspoons sugar
1 tablespoon butter

1 teaspoon sugar
¼ cup lukewarm water
1 tablespoon yeast
1 beaten egg
½ teaspoon grated lemon rind
2½ cups flour
½ cup butter soft enough to spread

Scald milk and add sugar and butter. Cool. Dissolve teaspoon of sugar in water and sprinkle with yeast. Allow to foam, about 10 minutes. Add egg, lemon rind and flour to make soft dough. Knead a little and put in buttered bowl to rise until doubled. Punch down and chill in refrigerator for 1 hour. Punch down again and roll out ¼ inch thick.

Divide butter in three equal parts and spread ⅓ on rolled dough. Fold ends of dough to center to make three layers. Roll again and spread with another ⅓ of the butter. Repeat. Fold over and chill for 1 hour.

Roll ¼ inch thick to rectangle. Cut in small squares. Place a teaspoon of filling on each square and fold to triangle, pinching edges to close firmly. Place on unbuttered sheet. Chill for 30 minutes. Brush with cream and bake at 400° for 15 minutes, then at 350° for 8 minutes.   Yield: 1 dozen

FILLING

½ cup raisins
½ cup currants
¼ cup chopped citron
1 cup sugar
¼ cup water
2 tablespoons flour
Grated rind and juice of one lemon
½ cup chopped walnuts

Combine and cook over low heat until thick. Take from stove and add walnuts. Cool before using.
                    Yield: 1½ cups

TEA DOWN UNDER

Robert Gaskin who often visits Australia recalls teas south of Melbourne.

"At 8:00 there is a big breakfast — hot or cold cereal; canned fruit, fried eggs, bacon, sausages, lamb chops or brains and tons of toast with jam, marmalade and tea.

"At 10:00, there is a tea with pumpkin scones, muffins, and whatever happens to be around. There is also pound cake cut in squares.

"Lunch consists of light cold cuts, salads and more tea. If there are sweets, they have fruitcake, sponge layer cake, pikelets or lamingtons.

"From 3:00 to 4:00, there is a big spread of everything you had at morning tea plus small sandwiches and more tea.

"When people asked me to come around for tea, they meant dinner at 6:00. This is a big meal with a 'joint,' potatoes, vegetables, and tea. Anyone still hungry after that could look forward to a supper about 9:30 or 10:00 with more tea, cakes and all the rest. The effect of eating like this all day long is devastating. But you must remember that Australians are hard workers and can use up all that energy."

In Australia, Mr. Gaskin has encountered everything from Lipton tea bags and ginger root tea to Billy Tea, an excellent black variety which lives up to its boast that it is famous. Its distinctive character appeals even to confirmed coffee drinkers.

A MEMORABLE TEA

Mr. Gaskin recalls having a ginger tea made by a Hindu woman to cure a cold. The tea burned a little on the way down, but it was very comforting. This is how you can make it. Strain before serving, of course!

GINGER INFUSION STRAIGHT

Steep 1 knob of freshly grated ginger root in 3 cups of water brought to a brisk boil. Treat as any other tea infusion. Serve with honey and lemon juice to taste.

BLACK TEA WITH GINGER ROOT

Infuse your favorite black tea in the usual way, adding grated ginger root to taste.

TEA FOOD RECIPES FROM AUSTRALIA AND FIJI

PUMPKIN SCONES

2 cups flour
3 teaspoons baking powder
½ teaspoon salt
2 tablespoons sugar
1 tablespoon melted butter
1 cup cooked, sieved pumpkin
1 egg

Sift dry ingredients together. In separate bowl, combine butter, pumpkin, and egg. Add to flour mix and mix lightly. If scone dough requires more liquid, add a tablespoon of light cream. Pat to ¾ inch thick on lightly floured board. Cut in squares or triangles. Sprinkle with sugar. Bake in quick oven until lightly browned, about 20 minutes. Serve hot with butter, honey or marmalade.

Yield: 1 dozen

PIKELETS

These pan cakes are great served with butter, strawberry jam; whipped cream and fresh strawberries; or creamed honey from Tasmania.

½ teaspoon soda
1 teaspoon cream of tartar
¾ cup milk
1 beaten egg
1½ tablespoons sugar
¾ cup flour

Combine soda, cream of tartar and milk. Pour onto beaten egg. Add flour and sugar to make creamy batter. Drop by spoonful on hot, lightly buttered frying pan. Cool and stack in air tight container until time to serve.

Yield: 6 large Pikelets

LAMINGTONS

Lamingtons are very popular tea cakes Down Under and they may try your soul before you are done with them. The best way to approach them is to arm yourself psychologically and repeat over and over, "I *can* make beautiful Lamingtons!" In any case, you can always depend on the coconut to cover any errors.

First make a yellow sponge cake as follows:

3 eggs separated
1 cup sugar
¼ cup hot water
1 cup flour
½ teaspoon baking powder
1 teaspoon vanilla

Combine egg yolks and sugar and beat well. Add beaten egg whites, then hot water and lastly flour sifted with baking powder, and vanilla.

Bake on buttered 11x7 inch sheet at 350° for 30 – 35 minutes. Cool on wire rack and cut into small squares. Dip each square in chocolate icing and roll in shredded coconut at once. Dry on rack.

CHOCOLATE ICING

Sift 1 lb. powdered sugar and 4–5 tablespoons cocoa into bowl. Add 4 tablespoons boiling water, 1 teaspoon butter and a few drops of vanilla. Stir until smooth and shiny. Use immediately. Keep bowl over hot water, adding a little hot water to icing if it begins to thicken.

Yield: 42 Lamingtons

A NECESSARY TEA SWEET

Marmalades are among the easiest bread spreads you can make successfully without having to boast any talent for the job. They are made from pulpy fruits, everything but core and seeds going into the pot.

You can make them bittersweet with a combination of lemons, oranges and grapefruit. Each fruit separately makes delicious marmalade, too. Other fruits that lend themselves to the marmalade pot are limes, ginger, kumquats, peaches, rhubarb, and combinations of carrots and oranges; cherries with lemon; green tomatoes with lemon; apricot with pineapple; pineapple with orange; and seedless grapes with orange.

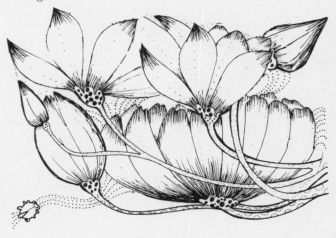

MARMALADE

Thinly slice 1 orange, 1 lemon and 1 grapefruit. For each cup of fruit, add 3 cups water and let stand overnight in glass bowl. Boil fruit rapidly until tender. Add 1 cup sugar for each cup of fruit mixture and liquid. Continue boiling until fruit is translucent and syrup sheets from spoon. Take from stove and hold for 5 minutes, stirring often to prevent fruit from floating. Fill jars to ¼ inch of top. When marmalade is cold and set, cover with paraffin. Store in cool, dry place.

Yield: Six 6-oz. glasses

AND THE GOOD TASTE OF LEMON

POUND CAKE

1 cup butter
1 cup sugar
1 teaspoon grated lemon rind
1 tablespoon lemon juice
5 eggs, unbeaten
2½ cups flour sifted with
½ teaspoon salt
1 teaspoon baking powder

Cream butter, sugar, lemon rind and juice until fluffy. Add eggs, one at a time, beating well after each addition. Add sifted dry ingredients, one-third at a time.

Put dough in 8x8 inch square pan lined with oiled brown paper. Bake at 325° until done, about 1 hour and a half. Cool on rack, wrap in waxed paper and hold for awhile before cutting.

Yield: 16 servings

BEST TEA DRINKERS IN THE WEST

Canadian tea drinkers lead all the rest in the Western Hemisphere.

In Winnipeg, Eaton's encourages them by providing a selection of tea sandwiches, grilled cheese squares, toasted asparagus rolls and an apple cake confection of tempting character. This is how to make two of these dishes.

ASPARAGUS ROLLS

Cut tops from small dinner rolls and scoop soft part out. Crisp the rolls in the oven. Fill with sauce.

Sauce: Make 1 cup of white sauce and add cooked asparagus tips and beaten yolk of 1 egg. Stir over fire until egg thickens. Squeeze in lemon juice to taste, season with salt and pepper. Fill rolls with sauce and garnish with parsley. Serve hot.

TOASTED APPLE CAKE

1½ cups flour
1 teaspoon baking powder
1 teaspoon baking soda
1 teaspoon salt
½ cup sugar

½ cup chopped walnuts
2 beaten eggs
¼ cup melted butter
½ cup water
½ cup all bran
1 cup chopped peeled apples
1 teaspoon vanilla

Sift dry ingredients together. Add nuts and remaining ingredients. Mix lightly. Spoon into buttered loaf pan. Bake at 350° 45 - 50 minutes. Cool on rack.

To serve, slice and toast one side under broiler. Turn slice and spread with ginger marmalade and return to broiler until marmalade bubbles. Serve at once heaped with whipped cream.

TEA IN VICTORIA

You can sit down to "Afternoon Teas and Delicacies" at the Nutshell in Victoria and have your choice of a dozen special teas. Delicacies include layer cakes; toasted crumpets with strawberry jam; toasted buns with raisins and cinnamon; and toast, dry or buttered, with honey or marmalade.

Tea cakes are rich. This buttermilk cake with walnuts is almost puddingy. It does very well with no glaze or frosting. It is enough to dust the top with powdered sugar. But you can bake this cake in layers, too, and frost.

ENGLISH WALNUT CAKE

½ cup butter
1 cup brown sugar
1 egg
1 cup buttermilk
2 cups flour
1 teaspoon soda
½ teaspoon baking powder
½ teaspoon salt
1 teaspoon ground cardamon
1 cup chopped walnuts

Cream butter and sugar; add beaten egg. Sift dry ingredients and add to batter alternately with buttermilk. Add walnuts last. Bake at 350° for 30 - 40 minutes in well buttered 9x9 inch pan. Cool on rack. Dust with powdered sugar.

Yield: 16 servings

CHERRY LAYER CAKE

¾ cup butter
1 cup powdered sugar
1¾ cups flour
2 teaspoons baking powder
¼ teaspoon salt
3 eggs well beaten
½ cup glacé cherries
¼ cup ground almonds
½ teaspoon almond extract
2 tablespoons water

Cream butter and sugar until fluffy. Add flour sifted with baking powder and salt. Add eggs, almond extract, water and almonds. Work to a smooth dough. Cut cherries in half, dredge with flour and add to dough. Bake in 8-inch cake pans lined with buttered paper. Bake at 350° for 30 - 40 minutes.

Cool on wire racks. Fill and frost layers with:

CHERRY GLAZE

3 tablespoons soft butter
1 egg yolk
Grated rind of ½ lemon
2 tablespoons cherry syrup from glacé cherries
2 cups powdered sugar

Thoroughly blend butter, yolk, lemon rind and cherry syrup. Add sifted sugar and stir until smooth.

LIGHT AS A FEATHER

Tea buns like these are sure to become family favorites. They merit the description of "tea delicacy" and are delicious served as they come from the oven, hot and sweet.

RAISIN-CINNAMON BUNS

1 tablespoon yeast
2 tablespoons lukewarm water
1 cup light cream
1 cup melted butter
3 eggs well beaten
1 cup sugar
4 cups flour sifted with 1 teaspoon each of powdered mace, cinnamon
1 cup raisins
Sugar for sprinkling

Dissolve yeast in water. Warm cream in double boiler. Remove from heat and stir in sugar and butter. Add eggs slowly, stirring constantly. Allow to cool a bit. Add foamed yeast to flour and spices. Stir in cream mixture and beat thoroughly to make smooth batter. Add raisins dredged in flour. Set dough to rise in warm place until double in bulk, about 3 hours.

Beat down and drop dough by tablespoon into well buttered muffin tins. Let rise in tins for another hour. Brush tops with mixture made of 1 egg beaten into ½ cup of milk. Sprinkle with sugar and bake at 375° for about 12 minutes.   Yield: 3 dozen+

TO EACH HIS OWN

Crumpets are so popular they have an international market. Italians sprinkle them with garlic. Japanese dip theirs in soy sauce. They come in all shapes and sizes — thick, thin, round, square (to fit your toaster), oval, and with and without holes. In 1973, five million were imported in the United States alone.

The first crumpets appeared in Victorian England at teatime. They were expensive — about 80 cents each by current reckoning. As late as 1963, crumpet men, balancing huge trays on their heads and ringing hand bells, hawked their wares in winter. They are no more.

Crumpets are "holey," the better to let the butter soak through. They appear at breakfast and afternoon teas with sweet butter, syrups, jams, jellies and marmalades. They are chewy, and until you have made them yourself, you have not had the best. Here's how!

CRUMPETS

1 teaspoon sugar
½ cup lukewarm water
1 tablespoon yeast
2 cups milk
½ cup butter
3–4 cups flour
¾ teaspoon baking soda
1 tablespoon hot water

Dissolve sugar in water and sprinkle with yeast. Let foam for 10 minutes. Scald milk and add butter. Cool to lukewarm and add yeast mixture. Beat in flour to make a soft dough. Cover and let rise until bubbly. Mix soda in hot water and beat into batter. Let dough rise until doubled.

Spoon ready dough into 3-inch crumpet rings on hot, buttered griddle. Cook until dry and bubbly on top. Remove rings and brown other side. Split and butter to serve.

Yield: 12

Note: You can make your own crumpet rings from empty 8 oz. fish or fruit cans by removing tops and bottoms.

AN-EASY-DOES-IT PLAN

You can *"can"* crumpets, too. Divide batter among two or three, well buttered, flour dusted one-pound coffee cans. Set to rise until double in bulk and bake at 375° for 1 hour. Cool and shake out finished loaves. Slice and toast. These are good for hot savory sandwiches you want to finish under the broiler. All crumpets we have made freeze very well.

TEA AT THE EMPRESS

Many tourists get into the spirit of things by having tea at The Empress. On the June day we were there, the menu offered English muffins and crumpets; assorted tea sandwiches; fresh Okanagan fruit salad with orange sauce; layer cake, and tea.

Most memorable was the setting. The lobby of this venerable institution was transformed into a tearoom. We sat at tables brought out for the tea and in chairs already there. Problems of mass service shadowed the gentility of the affair. We had to buy a ticket and stand in line. Anyone who came late had the prospect of seeing the whole portable equipage — tables, chairs and all — removed before his very eyes before he left!

What was truly lovely was the sight of so many whole families enjoying a leisurely tea, buzzing pleasantly and animatedly sharing the occasion. It was a good time. The motherly waitress was pleasant but not familiar. Dishes arrived in courses. The size of portions was so big, we left wondering how anyone could face dinner in another two hours.

The muffin recipe that follows makes an English version worthy of the title.

ENGLISH MUFFINS

    1 tablespoon yeast
    1 cup lukewarm water
    ½ cup scalded milk
    1 tablespoon sugar
    2 teaspoons salt
    4 cups flour
    ¼ cup soft butter
    White cornmeal

Dissolve yeast in water. Add milk cooled to lukewarm, sugar, salt and 2 cups of flour. Beat well and let rise in mixing bowl until double in bulk, about 1½ hours. **Beat in butter and remaining flour to make stiff dough. Knead on floured board 8 – 10 minutes and place in buttered bowl. Let rise in warm place until doubled, about 1 hour.**

Punch down and roll out ½ inch thick on board sprinkled with cornmeal. Cut with 3-inch cutter. Sprinkle tops with cornmeal. Place on sheet, cover and let rise another 30 – 40 minutes or until double in size. Bake on lightly buttered griddle at 325° for 25 minutes, turning several times. Cool on rack.

Yield 12 – 18 muffins

A MUFFIN POSTSCRIPT

A few years ago, bakery hucksters violated a sensitive tradition. Knowing what a hue and cry would ensue, they created an artificial controversy by planting the news that a "new" English muffin would be sliced by machine. A San Francisco newspaper obliged by reporting and a "multitude of muffin buffs were outraged to learn that these delicacies were to be put to the knife!"

Within two days, the bakery restored unsliced muffins at the same time it heavily advertised the new sliced variety. This marketing decision was hailed in the press as "a consumer victory of almost unheard of magnitude."

Whether the sliced muffins ever succeeded is of little consequence. But no one should be fooled: a real English muffin is properly pricked around its perimeter with the tines of a fork, then torn in half with the fork assisted by thumb and forefinger. It's the ragged surface of the muffin at the break that gives it its characteristic texture and distinctive flavor when it is toasted, which it must be. Serve your toasted muffins with butter, jam, preserves or honey, of course.

A PRIVATE TEA

With luck you might be invited to have tea in a private home in Victoria. If it should be with Elizabeth and Owen Goward, you could enjoy thinly sliced bread with butter, digestive biscuits, and raisin cake.

Mrs. Goward treasures the raisin cake recipe because she received it as a bride from the widow of Bishop Schofield. It is called Mrs. Thorpe-Double's Raisin Cake and it's pure English in character as well as in name.

MRS. THORPE-DOUBLE'S RAISIN CAKE

First boil 1½ cups raisins for 20 minutes in enough water to cover. Meanwhile, cream

1 egg
1 cup brown sugar
½ cup butter
1 teaspoon vanilla

Add the following dry ingredients:

1½ cups flour sifted with
  1 teaspoon cinnamon
  ½ teaspoon nutmeg
  1 teaspoon soda
  Pinch of salt

Add raisins to batter while hot. Bake in a square 8x8 inch pan at 350° for 30 minutes.

And Thinly Sliced Bread

If you start proofing this bread at 9:30 a.m., you will have it ready in time for late afternoon tea. It has a good crunchy crust and a finely textured body. Its taste is very satisfying — some of the best bread you will ever eat with sweet butter. This recipe makes a big dough. We use a very large crackled porcelain bowl for mixing and holding dough for rising because this beautiful stuff deserves the best!

ELIZABETH GOWARD'S WHOLE WHEAT BREAD

1 cup brown sugar
4 teaspoons salt
1 cup hot water
12 cups whole wheat flour
  (We substitute 3 cups of white for 3 cups of whole wheat)
1 teaspoon yeast
¼ cup lukewarm water
Enough additional water to knead easily, about 3 cups

Dissolve sugar and salt in hot water. Cool and pour into bowl with the 12 cups of flour. Make a little hole in the flour and put in the yeast with the lukewarm water. When yeast has risen, add enough water to knead easily, keeping dough on the wet side. Cover dough in bowl and let rise for 6 hours. Shape into three loaves, place in well buttered loaf pans and let rise until double in size. Bake at 350° for 1 hour.

Yield: 3 loaves

FIRST MAKE BREAD, THEN CAKE

While you are making Mrs. Goward's beautiful bread you can put aside a cup of dough from the second rising to make this interesting bun cake.

ENGLISH BUN CAKE

1 cup bread dough
   from second rising
½ cup mixed butter and
   lard
½ cup brown sugar
½ teaspoon cinnamon
¼ teaspoon nutmeg
¼ cup chopped seedless raisins
¼ cup currants, washed and dried
1 tablespoon minced citron

Cream shortening and sugar and beat in egg. Work into bread dough. Add spices and raisins, currants and citron dredged in flour. Knead vigrously for 3 or 4 minutes. To make a pretty loaf, you can press kneaded dough into a well buttered 7-inch brioche pan and let rise for 30 minutes or until well risen. Bake at 350°. Cool and serve as you would fruitcake.

GLORIFIED TOASTS

Now that you have beautiful homemade bread, you have many ways to make teatime toast one of the most satisfying of foods. You can invent your own spreads for toast and here are four suggestions to start.

CINNAMON SPREADS

Cream butter, cane or brown sugar, and cinnamon; or mix 2 teaspoons cinnamon with ½ cup of honey.

Toast bread in broiler. Spread mixtures on untoasted sides and return to broiler until spread bubbles.

COCONUT SPREAD

Cream equal parts of butter, powdered sugar, shredded coconut and add cinnamon to taste. Prepare toast as for cinnamon spread, above. Cut toast in strips to serve.

ORANGE SPREAD

Cream ½ cup butter, 3 tablespoons orange juice, 3 tablespoons sugar, 2 tablespoons grated orange rind. Add ground coriander or nutmeg to taste. Leftover spread keeps well in refrigerator.

WATERCRESS SPREAD

Wash and mince 1 bunch watercress. Add 2 tablespoons cream, 1 beaten egg, salt and pepper to taste, 1 tablespoon butter and a dash of lemon juice. Heat in sauce pan and stir until thick. Spread on hot buttered toast cut in squares; decorate with sprigs of watercress. Serve very hot.

A FAVORITE SPREAD

One of the best spreads for toast is the lemon curd or butter. An excellent commercial brand comes from New Zealand, but nothing will compare with fresh lemon butter you make yourself. It keeps well and goes happily on everything from toast to waffles as well as on tarts and as filling for layer cakes. A friend who enjoyed it for brunch thought it was as good as having lemon meringue pie without the meringue and crust!

LEMON BUTTER

3 eggs
1 cup sugar
5 tablespoons melted butter
2 lemons, grated rind and juice

Beat eggs and add sugar gradually, continuing to beat. Add butter, lemon juice and rind. Cook in double boiler until thickened, stirring constantly. Cool and store in refrigerator.

Yield: 1½ cups

TEA SANDWICHES

In a burst of pique, a critic vent his spleen on finger sandwiches "that fail to nourish." His criticism was unjust because they are not intended to fill. Their function is to beguile. After all, one doesn't have a tea to fill himself: He is only between meals and this is a time to try interesting foods and a time to talk.

Tea menus have included sandwiches with spreads of:

Caviar and every kind of cheese
Creamed chicken
Chicken and celery
Lobster, shrimp, smoked salmon, sardines, anchovies
Chicken and truffles
Lettuce, celery and coriander
Nuts
Cream cheese incorporating everything from chives to candied ginger, from slivered nuts to sliced fresh fruit
Grated apple and horseradish

The fillings and spreads are endless and you can have fun using every kind of bread — black, brown, white, rye, whole wheat, pumpernickel and breads made with fruit and cheese.

The tea sandwich is usually bite size and crustless, but even here you can be freewheeling and innovate. We happen to like crust and abhor the waste of it.

The more attractive and unusual tea sandwiches are, the more appealing will be the whole tea experience.

WHAT REALLY MATTERS, AFTER ALL

Old favorites, unexpected extravagances and homely fare rightly find their way to the tea table. It really doesn't matter whether they traditionally go with teas, although some do. What is most important is how you feel about them, for the real reason for a tea is to share something good to eat in the comfortable bosom of friends and family.

Here is a trio of such foods — one from Grandmother's cookbook; one that is usually associated with beans; and one that will drive you mad, perhaps!

GOOD FLOUR, GOOD PANS AND A HOT OVEN

"To make good gems, one must have good flour, a cast-iron pan, and a hot oven."

That was gospel according to "hygienic cooking" instructions in Grandmother's cookbook. To make the gems she used soft, cold water. She judged the amount of flour by the way it did or did not swell. She beat the batter fast and hard to get as much air in as possible. And she was careful not to squash the gems when she took them from the oven. She let no weight rest upon them.

But you will want something more definite to make these muffins with the very crisp and crusty outsides and moist, soft insides. You can make them this way.

GRAHAM GEMS

Combine and beat until light, about 4 minutes:

2 cups sour milk or buttermilk
1 teaspoon soda
1 egg
1 tablespoon light salad oil
½ teaspoon salt
2 tablespoons molasses
Graham flour, enough to make stiff batter

Bake in hot oven in buttered gem pans that are sizzling hot. Serve hot.

Yield: 18 gems

A VERSATILE, HEARTY PERFORMER

While steamed brown bread is more often associated with Saturday night bean suppers than with afternoon teas, it has a wide enough appeal to appear appropriately at both. This robust, old-time bread is delightful plain, buttered, or spread with cream cheese. For an out-of-this world taste, we like it sliced thin and topped with a wisp of chevre.

STEAMED BROWN BREAD

1 cup cornmeal
1 cup rye flour
1 cup Graham flour
2 teaspoons soda
1 teaspoon salt
2 cups buttermilk
¾ cup molasses
1 cup chopped raisins

Combine dry ingredients in bowl of electric mixer and stir well. Add floured raisins. Stir in buttermilk and molasses, mixing just enough to moisten batter well.

Line bottoms and sides of two well buttered one-pound coffee cans with waxed paper. Fill cans ⅔ full with batter. Cap cans with heavy duty

aluminum foil and secure with string. Place on a rack in deep kettle in 3 inches of boiling water. Cover kettle and let steam for 3 hours.

Remove cans from kettle and allow to cool a few minutes before turning breads out, still warm. When your Grandmother cut brown bread, she probably looped a string around a loaf and pulled the ends to arm's length. Bread freezes well. We serve both hot and cold.

Yield: 2 loaves

A LITTLE SCREAMING HELPS

Anyone who has devoted six months of his life to a study of Dostoevski will not be surprised to learn that when a Russian turns to baking, he does no ordinary thing. When we made these Russian yeast pastries for tea, there was confusion, noise and even despair in the kitchen. But the pastries were marvelous and stylish looking and we felt enormously rewarded for the effort.

RUSSIAN CHERRY TARTS

1 teaspoon sugar
½ cup lukewarm water
1 tablespoon yeast
2¾ cups flour
2 tablespoons sugar
½ teaspoon salt
½ pound chilled butter
1 egg

Jam or marmalade
Candied cherries, citron
Finely chopped walnuts
Beaten egg for glaze

Combine sugar and water and sprinkle with yeast. Let foam. Sift flour, sugar and salt. Grate butter with coarse grater. Combine with flour mix and keep cold.

Add beaten egg to yeast mix and add to flour mixture. Knead lightly but not until smooth; cover with waxed paper and chill for 1 hour.

Assemble enough jam, cherries, finely chopped walnuts to finish about 60 tarts. Whip egg for the glaze.

On floured board, roll dough ¼ inch thick. Cut in 2-inch squares. Put 1 teaspoon jam (apricot is nice) or your favorite marmalade mixed with chopped nuts in center of squares. Fold opposite corners to overlap at center. Place a cherry in open ends to close fillings. For contrast you can use cubed citron.

Arrange tarts on buttered sheet and chill for ½ hour. Brush with beaten egg and sprinkle with walnut.

Start in oven at 450° and turn back immediately to 375° to bake until lightly brown, about 10 – 12 minutes. Watch them. They burn easily.

Yield: About 60 tarts

Now, wasn't that fun?

INDEX OF RECIPES